VIRGINIA
— BY —
STAGECOACH

VIRGINIA C. JOHNSON

Published by The History Press
Charleston, SC
www.historypress.com

Copyright © 2019 by Virginia C. Johnson
All rights reserved

First published 2019

Manufactured in the United States

ISBN 9781467141017

Library of Congress Control Number: 2019937047

Notice: The information in this book is true and complete to the best of our knowledge. It is offered without guarantee on the part of the author or The History Press. The author and The History Press disclaim all liability in connection with the use of this book.

All rights reserved. No part of this book may be reproduced or transmitted in any form whatsoever without prior written permission from the publisher except in the case of brief quotations embodied in critical articles and reviews.

With gratitude and love to my husband, Steve, my best traveling companion down any stretch of road

And to my mother, Barbara Malone Crookshanks, who inspired me to discover and set down the past

CONTENTS

Acknowledgements	7
Introduction	9
I. How the Stagecoach Came to Be	11
II. The Royal Mail	19
III. Colonial Statesmen and the Road to Revolution	25
IV. Town to Town	42
V. A Night at a Coaching Inn	75
VI. The Golden Age of Stage Travel	87
VII. An American Way of Travel	94
VIII. A Visit to the Springs	102
IX. Dark Reflections	113
X. "If God Permits…": When Things Went Wrong	120
XI. The People Who Made Stagecoaches Work	132
XII. Heading South	140
XIII. Roads West	144
XIV. The Civil War	149
XV. The End of the Line	164
XVI. Traces of the Past You Can Visit Today	169
Sources	179
Index	185
About the Author	191

ACKNOWLEDGEMENTS

The author wishes to thank Mercy Sais of Central Rappahannock Regional Library for the many and timely interlibrary loans of research material; Elaine Shirley of Colonial Williamsburg Foundation for answering questions about its rare breeds program; the knowledgeable guides at Rising Sun Tavern and Michie Tavern; Anna and Daniel Cohen of Bay Haven Farm; L. Jagi Lamplighter Wright for the encouragement and cups of tea; and certainly Steve Johnson for always being willing (and able) to do what was needed to bring this project to fruition.

INTRODUCTION

The past is a foreign country: they do things differently there.

—L.P. Hartley, *The Go-Between*

When I first suggested writing a book on stagecoaches in Virginia, I was met with confusion from some quarters. Surely stagecoaches meant dusty drives through the sagebrush to deliver schoolmarms, broken-down gunfighters, the mail and sometimes even sacks of gold to meet payroll—all the plot elements a weekly Western needs.

Heathville (Heathsville) Tavern, Heathville (Heathsville), Northumberland County, Virginia, 1935. *Photograph by Frances Benjamin Johnston, courtesy of the Carnegie Survey of the Architecture of the South, Library of Congress.*

Introduction

Mrs. David Meade (Mary) Randolph, 1807. *By Charles Balthazar Julien Fevret de Saint-Mémin, courtesy of the Library of Congress.*

Who ever heard of stagecoaches back East? Well, everyone—everyone living in the late eighteenth and nineteenth centuries, at least. Stagecoaches, financed partially by the government as regular postal carriers, were a lynchpin of communication and general travel for first the colonies and later the young and growing republic.

As the country spread inland toward the mountains from the Eastern Seaboard, coaches that ran by stages, changing horses frequently (hence the term *stagecoach*), became a largely reliable connection between communities, and their need for places to rest, such as taverns and inns, gave rise to regular accommodations for the weary as well as all the practical services a traveler of the day might need, such as overnight housing, a blacksmith shop and certainly a vibrant tavern.

The coming of steam engines marked the end of stagecoaches as a primary means of travel between major cities, but for many decades after, until the rise of the automobile in the twentieth century, stagecoaches still connected farther-flung communities. Bringing stages up to meet the trains so that travelers could continue onward to the hinterlands—and make a connection for travelers heading to the city and other points passed by the railway—was a weekly if not daily occurrence.

In this small volume, we'll explore some of the history, scenarios and personalities that ran alongside the stagecoach trade. We'll also see what became of some of the inns and taverns that were part of the stagecoach network. With almost every community having at least one convenient stagecoach stop, there isn't any way to touch on all of them, just a representative few.

We'll close with places in Virginia where you can get a taste of older times, sometimes literally, as old and seemingly old taverns and inns offer comfortably modern hospitality with a historical flair. In keeping with that spirit, the beginning of every chapter will offer a recipe from Mary Randolph's nineteenth-century classic *The Virginia Housewife: Or, Methodical Cook*. Up-to-date versions of these favorites can be easily found, but the originals convey the challenges a hospitable cook might face when laying out platters to feed the hungry travelers.

I
HOW THE STAGECOACH CAME TO BE

POUND CAKE

WASH the salt from a pound of butter, and rub it till it is soft as cream—have ready a pound of flour sifted, one of powdered sugar, and twelve eggs well beaten; put alternately into the butter, sugar, flour, and the froth from the eggs—continuing to beat them together till all the ingredients are in, and the cake quite light: add some grated lemon peel, a nutmeg, and a gill of brandy; butter the pans, and bake them. This cake makes an excellent pudding, if baked in a large mould, and eaten with sugar and wine. It is also excellent when boiled, and served up with melted butter, sugar and wine.

Before European colonists arrived in what they would call Virginia, confederated tribes of Algonquian people, such as the Powhatan to the east and Siouan tribes mainly to the west, had their own ways of travel involving trails through forests and denser woods, valleys and along the Tidewater shores. Moving on foot or by water in canoes, their means of transportation were sufficient for how they had reaped the land and rivers. They had no horses or oxen pulling wide loads, so their frequented paths might be narrow. They lived full lives that, if not entirely peaceful, were sufficient and adapted through centuries, if not millennia.

The English touching on shore in the early 1600s would change all that, but it would take them years to do so. They brought horses on those voyages, but Jamestown's "Starving Time" would reduce them from noble helpers

Virginia by Stagecoach

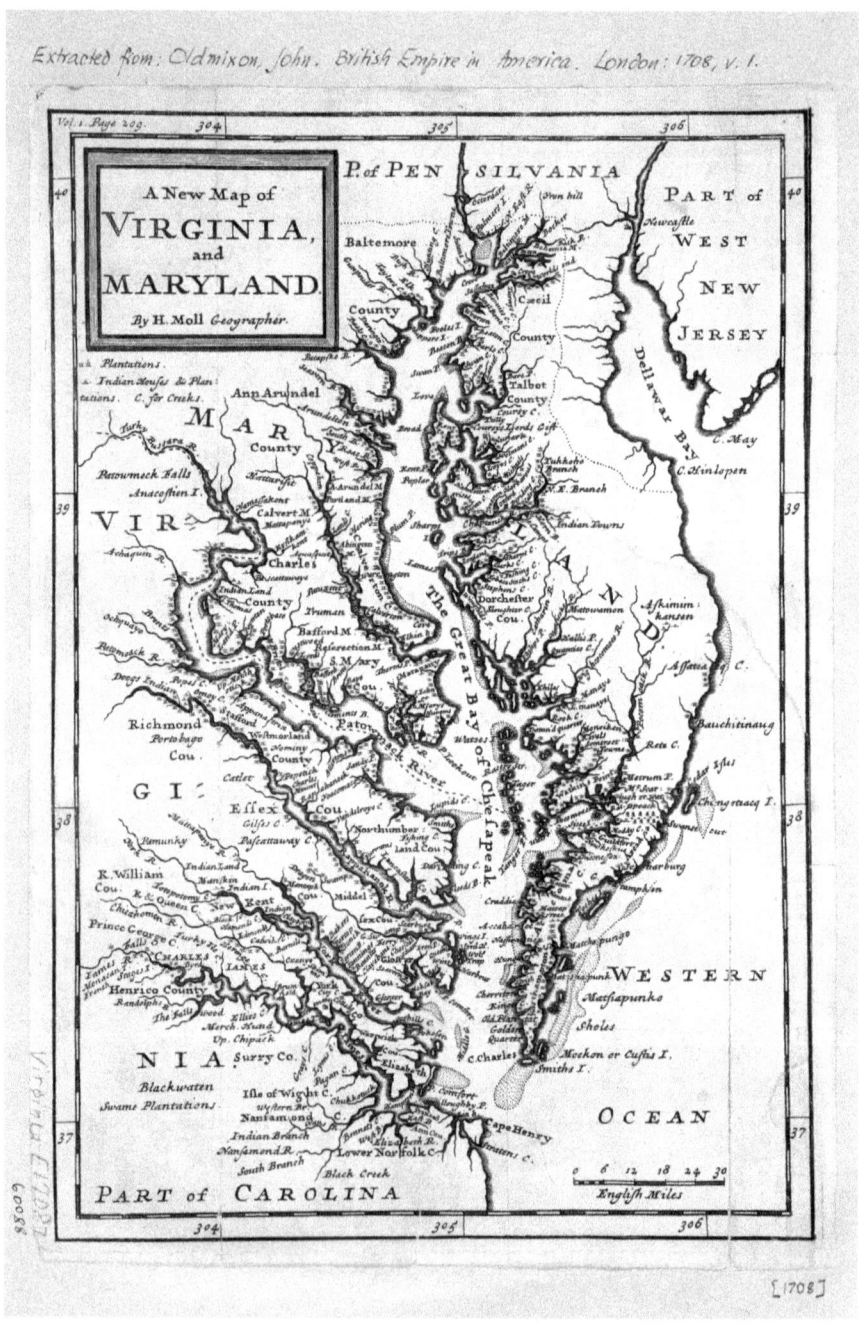

"A New Map of Virginia and Maryland," 1707, H. Moll, geographer. *Courtesy of the Lionel Pincus and Princess Firyal Map Division, New York Public Library.*

to a necessary food source. Through the following decades, the number of colonists increased, as did the number of horses.

At first, they employed the same paths and waterways as the tribes. An early map of the two Chesapeake Bay colonies of Virginia and Maryland is very much focused on the bay itself and its tributaries. Settlements were initially made along the Rappahannock, the James, the Potomac and the York Rivers, and river transport of goods and people, both locally and from the Old World to the New, was vital. They established forts at the headwaters of the rivers, traded with tribes and began to explore farther inland, usually with packhorses in tow hauling their gear.

THE COLONY GROWS

In time, both the ever-increasing new colonists and the enterprising established ones moved on in greater numbers to the interior, where there might be no pathways where they wanted them. Even if they existed, these trails would be insufficient to carry the products of their farming and mining to market.

Early two-wheeled carts and four-wheeled farm wagons might be built onsite, with wheels sometimes imported from England. Oxen were used more than horses to cart heavy loads.

By the beginning of the eighteenth century, horses were common. According to Francis Louis Michel, who visited Virginia from Switzerland in 1701 and 1702: "It must be a poor man who cannot afford one. Not many people can be seen traveling on foot, even if it is only an hour's distance. They are seldom used to draw wagons or the plow."

Thanks to the administrative efforts of the Virginia legislature—and more so the hard labor of its colonists—by 1700, roads were becoming established. The year 1632 brought the colony's first road law, whereby each county was to lay out roads in "convenient places." Laws also required each man to dedicate a certain number of hours per year working on those roads—either building or maintaining them personally or hiring another man to do the required job for him. This was a holdover from English feudal customs of yearly required work on one's master's land, which had become a matter for church parishes to administer and would have been familiar to the colonists. These laws, in one form or another, would remain in effect for the next 250 years.

THE MOST CONVENIENT WAYES

But how did they choose which way the roads should go? There were officials for that. In 1662, the Virginia General Assembly appointed "surveyors of the highways" to "lay out the most convenient ways to the church, to the court, to James Towne, and from county to county, and make the said wayes forty foot broad, and make bridges where there is occasion." Eventually, the required broadness of "said wayes" would be reduced to thirty feet, and the practical matters of laying out the roads would be handled locally through courts, a mirror of the British system.

The "overseers of the roads" or "surveyors of highways" were appointed annually by county courts. When an individual surveyor requested it, the parish vestry put out an order for all tithables (males above the age of sixteen whether free or slave) to go to work for the surveyor. A man who did not cooperate would be subject to a fine. A glance at order books during the colonial period shows a number of prosecutions for this, and a county court could be brought before a grand jury for refusing to do its duty by the roads.

In 1691, it became apparent that there was a need to build a road to connect the chain of frontier forts along the fall lines of the rivers so that they might communicate more easily with one another. Before the American Revolution, most colonial roads ran east–west, a famous one being Three Chopt or Three Notch'd Road, connecting the James River's fall line at Richmond to the Blue Ridge Mountains. It was first known as Mountain Road, incorporating an Indian trail and surveyed partially by Thomas Jefferson's father, Peter Jefferson, who also cocreated the Jefferson-Frye Map of 1751. Today, Route 250 and Interstate 64 follow that route, and as you get in closer to Richmond, you will see local roads still bearing the old name.

PAY THE FERRYMAN

Then there was the matter of the waterways. As the colony's first settlements were set along the banks of rivers, getting across them was a requirement for longer journeys. Crossing a broad river with livestock such as horses or oxen probably required a ferry, which, in many cases, might be just a crude raft. Ferries were so vital that the legislature tried to make them "free"—that is, being paid for by a tax—but small landowners objected, and the legislature opted to set a series of fees for travelers instead and grant the ferrymen tavern licenses to sweeten the deal. Ferrymen also got out of their required service in the militia and duty to maintain the roads. By the beginning of the eighteenth century, more than a dozen ferries crossed both the James and York Rivers. The Rappahannock River had six.

All of these transportation issues suggest that the colony wasn't ready to support something as regular and reliable as stagecoach traffic until well into the eighteenth century. Wealthy landowners might own lovely carriages mostly for town use, but a much more common way of getting an ordinary family or group some distance would be either on foot or on a practical farm wagon. Indeed, these early people-movers were made over a bit to become "stage waggons" once the idea of stage travel took hold.

Stagecoaches had been established in Britain for some time, with one of the first stage routes starting in 1610. By the end of the seventeenth century, stagecoaches ran three major routes in England, and some coaching inns served as theaters, such as the still-existing George Inn Theatre in Southwark, which saw performances of Shakespeare's plays.

THE START OF THE STAGECOACH

Americans certainly had an example to which to aspire, but the lower population density, rawness of the terrain, and not entirely calm relations with both native tribes and French colonials made for a less stable environment in which to run such a business. Even so, Oliver Wendell Holmes Sr., in his *Stagecoach East*, writes that there was a modest amount of staging in the East during the fifty years before the Revolution. Service was largely disrupted during the war, but as the British began to retreat and withdraw from various areas, a renewed and expanding stagecoach industry started to appear up and down the Eastern Seaboard.

By the 1750s, the major northern port cities of New York and Philadelphia had established stage lines connecting them, with stage-boats helping with water passages. Some stage lines ran as far south as Wilmington, North Carolina, according to the article "Stage Waggons and Coaches," written by Ron Vineyard for the Colonial Williamsburg Foundation. He notes that in the beginning of the eighteenth century, "stage coach" and "stage waggon" were used interchangeably, but, by the later eighteenth century, stage waggon was in favor, with stagecoach returning to common use with

Maryland waggon, 1777. *From* Coaches and Coaching Days: A Series of 50, *George Arents Collection, New York Public Library Digital Collections.*

the revolutionary coach redesigns of the early nineteenth century. Those first stage waggons were based on freight wagons and met with mixed reviews from passengers.

Francis Bailey wrote in his *Journal of a Tour in Unsettled Parts of North America, in 1796 & 1797*:

> *From Baltimore to Philadelphia are ninety-eight miles; between which places there is no want of conveyance, as there are three or four stages run daily. In one of these I place myself on the morning of March 3, 1796. A description of them perhaps would be amusing. The body of the carriage is closed in, about breast high; from the sides of which are raised six or eight small perpendicular posts, which support the covering—so that it is in fact a kind of open coach. From the top are suspended leather curtains, which may be either drawn up in fine weather, or let down in rainy or cold weather; and which button at the bottom. The inside is fitted up with four seats, placed one before the other; so that the whole of the passengers face the horses; each seat will contain three passengers; and the driver sits on the foremost, under the same cover with the rest of the company. The whole is suspended on springs; and the way to get into it is in front, as if you were getting into a covered cart. This mode of traveling, and which is the only one used in America, is very pleasant, as you enjoy the country much more agreeably than when imprisoned in a close coach, inhaling and exhaling the same air a thousand time over, like a cow chewing the cud; but then it is not quite so desirable in disagreeable weather.*

Vineyard writes:

> *The evolution from wagon to stagecoach is simple to follow. Benches or seats were first placed crosswise in the wagon box, and then a superstructure was constructed. The sides were made of either canvas or leather so they could be rolled up or down depending on the weather. As modifications were*

> made, the superstructure was suspended upon stout leather thoroughbraces that permitted play between the body and the undercarriage, and the bottom of the body became slightly rounded in the manner of a coach.

A private coach was prohibitively expensive for most people. Wealthy planter Robert Carter of Nomini Hall hired a tutor for his children who kept a very enlightening and often entertaining journal. Philip Vickers Fithian, the tutor, noted that in 1774 his employer took possession of a coach just arrived from England. Carter paid £120—enough, as noted in Colonial Williamsburg Foundation's *Rivers and Roads*, to pay for 800 gallons of rum or a journeyman's wages for four years.

But even before the establishment of stagecoaches, there was another option. Tavern keepers might rent horses and carriages to patrons—a very practical solution since visitors to town from the countryside, even if well-heeled, might not have any use for a carriage otherwise on rougher roads.

Vineyard goes on to reveal that the early "lumbering passenger and freight waggon, its bow-like canvas cover supported on hoops or tilts" was not designed by any means for passenger comfort but for carrying cargo first and people second, and it was up to the passengers to fit between boxes and barrels of merchandise. With springs and brakes lacking altogether, many preferred shanks' mare—that is, to go on foot—rather than endure the bone-jarring experience.

"A HARD WEEK'S TRAVEL"

In *Stagecoach Days and Stagecoach Kings*, the author notes that it was difficult enough for a man in breeches to climb aboard an early stage waggon, but a woman in full skirts would have to be boosted up by one pair of hands and hauled inside by another, crawling over plank seats until she reached the one assigned to her.

One thing is for certain, early stagecoaches did not run at the convenience of their passengers, whether they were well-known men or not. Future president John Quincy Adams's trip from Boston to New York in 1770 was no pleasure trip, as he wrote:

> *We generally reached our resting place for the night if no accidents intervened at ten o'clock and after a frugal supper, went to bed with a*

notice that we should be called at three in the morning which generally proved to be half past two, and then whether it snowed or rained the traveler must rise and make ready, by the help of a horned lantern and a farthing candle and proceed on his way over bad road sometime getting out to help the coachman out of a quagmire or rut. Finally arriving at New York after a hard week's travel wondering at the ease and the expedition with which our journey was affected.

It wouldn't be until the nineteenth century that public coaches' designs would become truly comfortable. In the meantime, there were plenty of rough roads and sore passengers. But the need to connect the colonies and later the new states by regular mail routes led to the development of north–south roads, better facilities all around and eventually what became known as the golden age of stagecoaches from the 1820s to the 1840s.

A MORE CAVALIER APPROACH

While sober-minded, religious persons made up the bulk of colonists in New England, the eastern part of the Virginia colony was another matter altogether. The cavaliers, loyal to King Charles II rather than Cromwell's rule, flocked here, bringing with them their affinity for good times. That was reflected in their public lodging as well. According to Elise Lathrop's *Early American Inns and Taverns*, at their ordinaries, billiard tables might be provided, with a bowling alley along the side.

Dancing, gambling and, of course, drinking were regular activities that might be enjoyed by travelers and locals as well. But that is not to say that taverns were regarded by the general population as dens of iniquity. On the contrary, owning and running an ordinary could be something in which to take pride.

As recorded in *Early American Inns and Taverns*, early English traveler Mrs. Wakefield observed, "We can scarcely pass ten or twenty miles without seeing an ordinary. They all resemble each other, having a porch in front, the length of the house, almost covered with handbills. They have no sign. These Virginia taverns take their name from the person who keeps the house, who is often a man of consequence."

II
THE ROYAL MAIL

PEACHES IN BRANDY

GET yellow soft peaches, perfectly free from defect and newly gathered, but not too ripe; place them in a pot, and cover them with cold weak lye; turn over those that float frequently, that the lye may act equally on them; at the end of an hour take them out, wipe them carefully with a soft cloth to get off the down and skin, and lay them in cold water; make a syrup as for the apricots, and proceed in the same manner, only scald the peaches more.

It wasn't until stagecoaches started officially (and profitably) delivering mail that timely service became a priority, and profits became less market-driven. But that would be a long time in coming, both because the state of colonial roads could only support individual riders and because of Virginia's strong resistance to change.

A regular mail service was seen, certainly by the Crown, as vital to maintaining and promoting businesses, and the king was willing to pay for it. As a colony, Virginia was quite late in becoming a part of the Royal Mail service. While New York, East and West Jersey, Pennsylvania, Delaware and New England all became party to the unified system by the 1690s, both Maryland and Virginia held out longer—in Virginia's case, much longer.

LATE AT THE POST

Why the delay? Virginia had been relatively content with relying on tobacco ships and inter-coastal schooners to unofficially get its mail to England and back and around the colonies. It was in no wise an official system, which is to say there was no pre-established fee to be paid and no set schedule.

Even with no agreement in hand signed off on by the Virginia House of Burgesses, resident deputy postmaster Andrew Hamilton of New Jersey appointed Peter Heyman, local collector of customs for the Lower James River, to be his deputy for the colony. But insurmountable arguments on both sides, mainly involving how much could be charged for a piece of mail to be carried, left Virginia without official postal service for a generation. Peter Heyman would never be the Virginia colony's postmaster. He was killed in action in 1700 against a French pirate, Louis Guittar, in Lynnhaven Bay as he stood on deck of "ye king's Shippe *Shoreham*" next to pistol-wielding Virginia governor Sir Francis Nicholson.

Meanwhile, the colony continued without regular postal service. As lieutenant governor in 1717, Alexander Spotswood announced that certain postal lines were "settled" in Virginia, but that wasn't the reality. Certain of the plantation owners had set out to block him, and they did so effectively. It wasn't until he retired as lieutenant governor and was taking more of an interest in his mining activities that, while on a business trip to London in January 1729/30, he happened to be called in by the royal treasury. (The old English calendar, in common use until 1751, pegged the new year as

Colonial post rider, 1673. *Courtesy of the Federal Highway Administration, Library of Congress.*

beginning March 25, or "Lady Day," so called for "the Annunciation of our Lord to the Blessed Virgin Mary," as remembered by the Church of England.) He was appointed deputy postmaster general and given the management of the American posts for ten years.

On November 3, 1737, the *Pennsylvania Gazette* contained the following advertisement:

> *Notice is hereby given that the Post Office in Philadelphia is now kept at B. Franklin's in Market Street, and that Henry Pratt is appointed Riding Post Master for all the stages between Philadelphia and Newpost in Virginia, who sets out about the Beginning of each month and returns in 24 Days, by whom Gentlemen, Merchants, and others may have their Letters, etc. carefully conveyed and Business faithfully transacted, he having given good security for the same to the Hon. Col. Spotswood, Post Master General of all his Majesty's Dominions in America;*

On April 28, 1738, the *Virginia Gazette* supplemented this with a more extended announcement:

> *Alexander Spotswood, Esq., Sole Deputy Post-Master-General of America, having formed a new Regulation for carrying on the Several Post Stages with Greater Expedition and Certainty than hitherto…*
>
> *The Post is set off from the General Post Office at New Post, on Wednesday, the 26th, inst. To cross over the Potowmack that night, and arrive at Annapolis on the Friday; there he is to make some stop and then proceed to Susquehanna, where he is to arrive on Saturday night; and to exchange Mails with the Philadelphia Rider, who is there to meet him. The Monday following, he is to return to Annapolis and arrive at Patowmack on the Tuesday night, from whence the Mail is to be brought to New Post, on the Wednesday, and the next morning to set out for Williamsburg, where he is to arrive on Saturday.*

THE GOVERNOR PREVAILS

Spotswood's "General Post Office at New Post" was on his land on the south side of the Rappahannock below Fredericksburg at the mouth of Massaponax Run. Judge Alvin T. Embrey, in 1923, noted:

> *On it was the eastern terminus of the Mine Road which Gov. Spotswood had cut through the forest from the river to his mine and on it also to this day, very near the confluence of the creek with the river, are the foundations of old buildings. What is known as the Tidewater Trail, from Fredericksburg down the Williamsburg way goes through the farm.*

The local tradition is that the ancient Potomac Path, which leads north from Fredericksburg to Alexandria, was known as early as the middle of the eighteenth century as the King's Highway, likely so called after it became a postal route. Spotswood served as deputy postmaster general for ten years, dying in 1740.

Good as it was to have a postal service established, tying the colonies together, Spotswood's endeavor relied on post riders, who had their limits both in what could be carried and potential side benefits for travelers. Both public and privately engaged post riders continued to serve.

A BLACKSMITH HAMMERS OUT A DEAL

Until Captain Levi Pease convinced the fledgling U.S. Post Office Department that the mail service would be safer and faster if provided by stagecoach, the very young nation's mail was still carried entirely by post riders. The needed act was passed in 1785, and Pease received the first mail contract ever given and made the first delivery by stagecoach in January 1786. From then until the 1840s, when the telegraph and the trains gained prominence, the stagecoach was the main artery of communication for the United States.

Who was this highly influential individual? Levi Pease (1740–1824) was a blacksmith and a Revolutionary War veteran who had been in charge of delivering horses, artillery, and supplies to Continental troops, including securing them for the final battle at Yorktown.

After the war, he began a small stage line in his home state of Connecticut that he soon expanded to Boston and farther down the Eastern Seaboard, using those less-than-comfortable stage waggons. Even so, Pease was an innovator who hired conductors to issue tickets and handle money—taking the business portion out of the hands of the drivers—and offered more direct routes for a higher fee for customers willing to pay. By the end of the 1700s, Pease's coaches carried mail (and passengers) on routes from New Hampshire to Georgia.

When he retired from the stagecoach business, selling his share to his partner, he took on the new and important role of establishing turnpikes. These roads, funded by travelers themselves, could provide citizens with better-maintained routes on which to journey. In this later chapter of life, Pease became known as the "Father of the Turnpike," and his well-maintained turnpikes reduced mail delivery times between New York and Boston from six days to thirty-six hours.

Now that the government-paid mail runs were helping to subsidize passenger coaches, there could be more of them, and other stagecoach operators also prospered. However, influential as he was, Levi Pease was not the only stagecoach operator with a federal contract running lines through the Old Dominion.

A HAZARD TO PROGRESS

The stagecoach-as-mail-carrier began under Postmaster Ebenezer Hazard's administration, but he was quite concerned with the bottom line, and, when the New York–to–Boston stagecoach route became less profitable, he replaced the stages for a time with post riders. This had the effect of curtailing the low-cost—if not free—delivery of newspapers, as post riders simply had no room to carry them. As the finer points of the Constitution were being actively debated in the press, this was a most awkward time to limit citizens' access to newspapers. George Washington was particularly vexed, and Hazard's days on the job were numbered.

George Washington clearly saw the need to expand viable stagecoach routes, as he wrote in this letter to Sir Edward Newenham dated March 20, 1785:

> *From the Southern parts of this State* [Virginia], *say from Norfolk, thro' Hampton, Richmond, Fredericksburg, and Alexandria which is within a few miles of this place* [Mount Vernon], *there is a regular Stage which passes thrice every week, it is neither of the best or worst kind. From Alexandria thro' the Metropolis of every State, Annapolis in Maryland excepted, which is a little to the right of the Post Road which goes thro' Baltimore. There is also a regular Stage to Portsmouth in New Hampshire, they are of a similar kind, and pass as often as those first mentioned; so that not more than three intervening days can happen between one Stage day and*

another. A person may therefore, at any time between the first of April and first of December, travel from Richmond (the metropolis of this State) to Boston, in ten or twelve days; and return in the same time. Between this State and Charleston, South Carolina no Stages are as yet established, and the country for the most part being poor and thinly inhabited, accommodations of every kind, I am told are bad. So much for public convenience; and I do not think I should deceive you much, was I to add that Sir Edwd. Newenham would find no difficulty to be accommodated, in this and some other States, with horses and carriages of private gentlemen, from place to place where inclination or business might induce him to go.

Yet within a decade or two, the growing country would have ample stage transportation connecting its major cities. Before we move on to that, however, let's pause to take a look at the importance of early coaching routes—and their taverns—during the time of the American Revolution.

III

COLONIAL STATESMEN AND THE ROAD TO REVOLUTION

GINGER WINE

To three gallons of water, put three pounds of sugar, and four ounces of race ginger, washed in many waters to cleanse it; boil them together for one hour, and strain it through a sieve; when lukewarm, put it in a cask with three lemons cut in slices, and two gills of beer yeast; shake it well, and stop the cask very tight; let it stand a week to ferment, and if not clear enough to bottle, it must remain until it becomes so; it will be fit to drink in ten days after bottling.

Although stagecoaches were not yet regularly active in Virginia by the time of the American Revolution, there were plenty of inns and taverns already in existence that would certainly continue to serve an expanded clientele once the stages started to run after the war.

Taverns were gathering spots where supper—and libations—could be enjoyed. A tavern might be the literal stage for a traveling theater performance, and the larger ones hosted dances and other community events. They were also the places where local gentry could meet to form jockey clubs. The clubs would set the racing schedules at local tracks, which might be attached to the taverns themselves.

In such a comfortable and social atmosphere, it was only natural that the colony's leaders would feel free to discuss other matters of interest to them—such as the rising feelings of rebellion.

"A BAR-KEEPER" FANS THE FLAMES OF LIBERTY

One of the Virginia colony's fieriest orators got his start at a tavern. Patrick Henry was born in Hanover County. His father was an educated man from Aberdeenshire, Scotland, who immigrated to America and married a wealthy widow. However, the wealth would not pass on to Patrick, as his elder half-brother stood to inherit, and he had many sisters who must be provided for as well.

To save money, his father withdrew him from formal schooling before he finished and set him up to run a store and maintain himself in that way. Having no experience—and an incomplete education—it is not surprising that the store failed. Then, still a teenager, Patrick married Sarah Shelton. Her father gifted his new son-in-law six slaves and a worn-out three-hundred-acre farm. Patrick worked alongside the slaves trying to clear fresh ground, but Virginia was experiencing a severe drought that lasted for some years, and the farm failed. After their house burned down, Patrick accepted a job working at his father-in-law's Hanover Tavern.

Hanover Tavern is located across the road from the courthouse, as was common in many communities. Attorneys were frequent customers. Impressed by Patrick's intelligence, they convinced him to try his hand at law. Today, that might seem an impossible proposition, as he needed to keep working to support his growing family and had no higher schooling. But in those days, it was not uncommon for would-be lawyers to "read law under" established attorneys, memorizing the contents of thick law books. Once a student felt himself ready, he could take examinations and, if he passed, become an attorney. This is still technically possible today in Virginia, although it is rarely done.

Patrick Henry had to do it with borrowed books that he read at night, as he had to work at Hanover Tavern during the day. After a short time studying, he hied himself to Williamsburg, where his knowledge was examined at length by three of the best-known attorneys of the day in separate interviews. He impressed them—well, two out of three of them, anyway. But that was enough. He passed.

He went on to become a noted revolutionary and a passionate attorney who derived much of his style from evangelical preachers favored by his mother and who sometimes argued cases against much better connected—and formally educated—men. This included Thomas Jefferson, who developed a real dislike for him. Although both went on to become governors of Virginia, Jefferson never forgot his fellow patriot's humbler background and did not hesitate to mention to friends that Patrick Henry got his start as "a bar-keeper."

Left: Patrick Henry. *Courtesy of the Thomas Addis Emmet collection, Manuscripts and Archives Division, New York Public Library.*

Below: Old Tavern, Hanover County, Virginia, 1935. *Photograph by Frances Benjamin Johnston, courtesy of the Carnegie Survey of the Architecture of the South, Library of Congress.*

Hanover Tavern, where Patrick Henry got his start. *Author's photograph.*

Patrick Henry, unlike some of the more prosperous patriots, had a deep understanding of the daily trials of ordinary men and was known for his personal hospitality that cut across class lines. Today, you can tour both Hanover Tavern, where he got his legal start, and nearby Scotchtown, his home during those years of revolution.

WASHINGTON'S FRIEND, COMRADE-IN-ARMS AND TAVERN KEEPER

Fredericksburg, home to several members of George Washington's family, was a frequent stop for the supreme commander of the Continental army. His boyhood days were spent there, and he had numerous friends in the neighborhood who shared his revolutionary sentiments, including William Fitzhugh of Chatham.

George Weedon, owner of Weedon's Tavern in Fredericksburg, had served under Washington during the French and Indian War in the 1750s. Weedon assumed management of the tavern about 1764; it was previously known as Gordon's Tavern and was owned by his wife's family. Weedon's Tavern was one of Washington's favorite places to frequent, as is noted in his journals.

He found it a convenient place to meet friends and officers of Virginia's troops. Dinner (taken mid-day in the South) once lasted until after sunset, and he might well be up for a game of cards. He reported on one event where he "lost as usual" and was afraid those Fredericksburg fellows were "too smart" for him.

George Weedon's sister-in-law married Hugh Mercer, a physician and Scottish refugee. He was at the Battle of Culloden, where he served as an assistant surgeon to "Bonnie Prince Charlie" Stuart. Both Weedon and Mercer would become generals in the Continental army, and after Mercer's heroic death at the Battle of Princeton, his brother-in-law naturally looked after his family.

Hugh Mercer had met Washington during the French and Indian War, where the young doctor took up ministering to the British wounded. He later joined the army of Continental soldiers, survived a journey across the wilderness while wounded, and was promoted to colonel, ultimately commanding garrisons. Mercer moved to Fredericksburg in 1760 and became a prosperous businessman. The Hugh Mercer Apothecary Shop can be visited today, and the Hugh Mercer Monument, including a full-body portrayal with sword drawn, is a few blocks away on Washington Avenue.

OFF TO THE RACES—AND THE REVOLUTION

But back to Weedon's Tavern. It was a place where lottery tickets might be bought to finance the building of a new church, but it was a particular mecca for the gathering of sportsmen. Behind his tavern, Weedon kept stables where gentlemen might board their purebred horses during the Fredericksburg Jockey Club's regular races at the fairgrounds.

The *Virginia Gazette* on September 16, 1766, announced that the horses to be run in the Fredericksburg Races were "to be entered, shown, and measured at Captain George Weedon's on the Monday preceding the races." George Weedon was the secretary of the Fredericksburg Jockey Club, the majority of whose races were open to members only.

According to George Harrison Sanford King's article "General George Weedon," Weedon's Tavern was the favorite meeting place of such patriots as George Washington, Thomas Jefferson, Patrick Henry, Hugh Mercer, George Mason, John Marshall, Richard Henry Lee and others.

George Weedon left his tavern to another to manage when the Revolution began so that he might offer his services. He rose from lieutenant colonel to brigadier general over the course of the war. He served alongside Lafayette and led the Virginia militia at Gloucester Point during the siege of Yorktown.

After the Revolution, General Weedon returned home to a stately house called the Sentry Box, still standing on lower Caroline Street. He was very much respected by his fellow Virginians. Indeed, in 1785, young Colonel (later President) James Monroe wrote to ask his advice on acquiring a home in town for him and his future bride. On his advice, Monroe and Weedon soon became neighbors. The James Monroe Law Office can be visited in town.

In later years, Weedon rented out his tavern to other tavern keepers, and it remained a center for "large entertainments," including hosting dinners in honor of special guests, often heroes of the Revolution. Following in Weedon's footsteps, new proprietor John Benson kept up the hospitality as well as offering a livery stable where horses might be rented. He was the postmaster, too, calling his venture the Old Stage Office.

RENDEZVOUS AT THE RISING SUN

Although Weedon's Tavern is no longer standing, Fredericksburg visitors can get a sampling of tavern life at the Rising Sun Tavern. Originally built as a private residence in 1760 by George Washington's brother Charles, it was sold and became a tavern in 1792, just in time for business to pick up from the mail stagecoaches. It operated as a tavern for thirty-five years. The building was acquired by the Association for the Preservation of Virginia Antiquities at the turn of the twentieth century and is now cared for by Washington Heritage Museums.

The first floor has a large room for the gentlemen, a separate parlor for the ladies and a taproom for the common folk, complete with barred cage to protect the staff—and the liquor—from drunken rowdies. This small museum, filled with authentic and period furnishings, has everything from a communal punch bowl shared by the gentry to plain pallets on the floor for common men to mousetraps to keep all the clientele from being gnawed upon during the night. The tour is lively, and Washington Heritage Museums feature special events at their properties most months of the year that explore period customs and local legends in detail.

Fredericksburg Tour, Rising Sun Tavern, 1920. *Courtesy of the National Photo Company Collection, Library of Congress.*

Rising Sun Tavern, Tap Room, Fredericksburg, Virginia, 1927–29. *Photograph by Frances Benjamin Johnston, courtesy of the Carnegie Survey of the Architecture of the South, Library of Congress.*

Virginia by Stagecoach

Raleigh Tavern's Apollo Room. *From* The Pictorial Field-Book of the Revolution, vol. 2, *by Benson Lossing, 1860 edition.*

MEANWHILE, IN THE COLONIAL CAPITAL...

Over at the Raleigh Tavern in May 1769, the kettle of sedition was simmering nicely. Members of the Virginia House of Burgesses had spoken out in protest of the 1767 Townsend Acts, which put a tax on imported china, glass, lead, paint, paper and tea. Royal Governor Lord Botetourt dissolved the Burgesses, and they chose to reconvene in the Apollo Room of the nearby Raleigh Tavern. It was a comfortable place for the gentlemen, festooned with a bust of Sir Walter Raleigh, and the Latin motto *Hilaritas sapientiae et bonae vitae proles* ("Jollity is the offspring of wisdom and good living") was written over the mantel.

THOMAS JEFFERSON, LOVE-STRUCK SWAIN

In happier times, the Apollo Room was the scene for dances and other courtly entertainments. Indeed, as a student at William & Mary, young Thomas Jefferson recounted his courtship of one Rebecca Burwell (whom he called "Belinda") there in 1763. It did not go as he hoped:

In the most melancholy fit that ever any poor soul was, I sit down to write to you. Last night as merry as agreeable company and dancing with Belinda in the Apollo could make me, I never could have thought the succeeding Sun would have seen me so wretched as I now am. I was prepared to say a great deal. I had dressed up in my own mind such thoughts as occurred to me, in as moving language as I know how, and expected to have performed in a tolerably creditable manner. But, good God! when I had an opportunity of venting them, a few broken sentences, uttered in great disorder, and interrupted with pauses of uncommon length, were the too visible marks of my strange confusion.

MAKING FRIENDS IN OTHER COLONIES

Important though less personal matters were also in play in 1769, and the burgesses who reconvened at the Apollo Room decided to form a nonimportation association in protest.

The House of Burgesses was reconvened in the fall, but the sparks had not gone out. Just a few years later in 1773, at Richard Henry Lee's suggestion, lawmakers Thomas Jefferson, Patrick Henry, Francis Lightfoot Lee, and Dabney Carr met again at the Apollo Room, this time with a plan to form a committee of correspondence to circulate letters between themselves and the angry legislatures of the other colonies.

On May 27, 1774, Royal Governor Lord Dunmore dissolved the House of Burgesses once more when it objected to British troops closing the Port of Boston after the Tea Party protest. This time, eighty-nine burgesses gathered at Raleigh Tavern and wrote up another nonimportation agreement, drafted by George Mason and introduced by George Washington.

While the original Raleigh Tavern cannot be visited today, as it burned down in 1859, Colonial Williamsburg Foundation rebuilt the structure as part of its efforts to recreate the historic district of the colonial capital. It certainly captures the building's spirit, right down to the gilt-lettered motto over the mantel.

A PRIME LOCATION

Opposite Raleigh Tavern stands Wetherburn's Tavern. It was another place that was filled to the brim when the Virginia General Assembly

A recreation of Josiah Chowning's tavern in Colonial Williamsburg. *Author's photograph.*

was in session. Its proprietor, Henry Wetherburn, had married Mary Bowcock, the widow of the owner of Raleigh Tavern, in 1731. He managed Raleigh's handily for a time. Peter Jefferson, Thomas Jefferson's father and a famous mapmaker, was a customer. In 1738, Wetherburn purchased adjacent lots across the street, presumably to build a house, but when a group of men purchased Raleigh Tavern, he opened Wetherburn's Tavern in his new home.

After Mary died in 1751, Henry Wetherburn married another widow of a tavern owner. Anne was the widow of James Shields and daughter of tavern keeper John Marot. When Henry Wetherburn died, Anne did not remarry but petitioned to receive her widow's share—one third of the estate. She was awarded the tavern. The tavern's twentieth-century restoration was aided immensely by the detailed inventories that were made during colonial times.

HANDY TO THE ENCAMPMENT

Farther west, Boswell's Tavern (ca. 1753) was owned by the Scotsman John Boswell. During the American Revolution, both the British and the Continental armies camped nearby, and it was a stopping place for James Madison, Thomas Jefferson, James Monroe and the Marquis de Lafayette. Boswell's Tavern, located near Gordonsville, is now a private residence.

Major General François de Chastellux, a French officer who had served under General Rochambeau during the American Revolution, arrived late one evening at Colonel Boswell's tavern and found Boswell "ill prepared to receive strangers." Supper was "rather frugal" but "breakfast the next morning was better; we had ham, butter, fresh eggs, and coffee with milk to drink."

A look at Boswell's Tavern reveals interesting patterns that repeat in the history of these old structures. When John Boswell died in 1788, the tavern was the hub of several of his properties, including farm sites, a mill and a blacksmith's shop. Eight hundred acres in total, the whole of it was maintained by fifty slaves.

The tavern remained "Boswell's" for twenty years after his death, as it was managed by John Boswell's widow. In 1802, the tavern was sold to Ludlow Branham, and it is as Branham's Tavern that readers will find it in the historical records. As happened with so many taverns as modes and ways

Coach and driver in Colonial Williamsburg. *Author's photograph.*

Boswell's Tavern, near Mechanicsville, Louisa County, Virginia, 1935. *Photograph by Frances Benjamin Johnston, courtesy of the Carnegie Survey of the Architecture of the South, Library of Congress.*

of transport changed, it became a private residence, selling off its tavern bar to Colonial Williamsburg during the Depression.

VIRGINIA'S PAUL REVERE

Another nearby watering hole, the Cuckoo Tavern (no longer standing) played a particularly gripping part in the Revolution as the starting point for Jack Jouett's ride. New England may have Paul Revere, but in the Old Dominion, a tavern keeper's son rode to similar fame in 1781. Jack Jouett and his father had signed Albermarle County's declaration in opposition to the English king. His loyalties were without question, so when he happened to overhear a plan by the British Army, led locally by dreaded Colonel Banastre Tarleton, to seize the Virginia governor (then Thomas Jefferson) from his home at Monticello, Jouett was determined to warn him—and the rest of the Virginia legislature who were meeting nearby in Charlottesville.

Jouett set off at night for a forty-mile ride using trails and old roads to reach the legislators in time. This he did successfully, first finding Jefferson and some of the legislators at Monticello and then riding two more miles to his father's Swan Tavern (also no longer standing) in Charlottesville. Most of the legislators got away and were able to reconvene in Staunton a few days later. For his service, the strapping six-foot-four, 220-pound Jouett was awarded a pair of pistols and eventually a sword.

TO SUPPORT THE PATRIOT CAUSE!

From whence did the various beers, ciders and liquors come that were sold in taverns? The Shenandoah Valley was known for its agriculture, and part of that agricultural produce could be turned into spirits to sell. The names of the revolution-minded citizenry who sold their produce in bottled form to the new government "to support the Patriot Cause" are recorded in court records of the day, and some are gathered in "Spirits, Stills, and Temperance: Tracing the History of Alcohol in Shenandoah County." Among those contributing were Gasher Branner (thirty-two gallons of whiskey), Ann Muhlenberg (seventy gallons of brandy—possibly from the farm her minister husband managed), Henry Funk (thirty-four gallons of brandy), George Huttle/Hottel (sixty-six gallons of whiskey), George Bird (fifty-two gallons of whiskey) and L. Snapp (one hundred gallons of whiskey).

AFTER THE REVOLUTION

Prior to the American Revolution, the best-established stage routes were the New Jersey routes, the Delaware-Maryland peninsula routes, the Boston–to–New York route and the local lines radiating out from the three hub cities of Boston, New York and Philadelphia. As the British captured these areas, service naturally ceased, but as the years passed and the British were driven out, stage lines resumed their business.

Once peace was declared and the existing stage lines came into their own again, others were started to tie all of the new states together along what was called the Main Post Road, which ran south from Wiscasset, Maine, through the leading seaboard cities to Savannah, Georgia. According to Oliver Wendell Holmes Sr., writing in *Stagecoach East*, it would remain the main route until the start of the National Road in 1818.

The rather democratic nature of the stagecoach, as it was run in America, did not go unnoticed by visiting Europeans. They may not have cared for the style of the coach's turn-out or the roughness of the roads, but some of them did find something uniquely positive about this very American mode of transport.

A FRENCHMAN IS IMPRESSED

Jacques Pierre Brissot de Warville (1754–93) was a leader of the Girondins, a pro-revolutionary group in France that would be among the first to be executed by bloodier-minded forces of the Montagnards and the Sans Culottes during France's Reign of Terror. Before their elimination, the Girondins had been instrumental in turning over power from the royalty and aristocrats to the common people. They also had hopes of spreading the revolutionary fervor to other nations by military means. Thomas Paine, British-born American activist and author of *Common Sense*, was an ally to the Girondins, whose political base was southwest France's Gironde region.

In any event, this soon-to-be-revolutionary Frenchman was just another person riding the early American stage in 1788. The fall of the Bastille would not happen until the following year. Not surprisingly, his observations dovetailed nicely with his politics, and he found the experience a positive one:

> *You find in these stages men of all positions. They succeed each other with rapidity. One who goes but twenty miles, yields his place to one who goes farther. The mother and daughter mount the stage to go ten miles to dine; another stage brings them back. At every instance, then, you are making many new acquaintances. The frequency of these carriages, the facility of finding places in them and the low and fixed price, invite the Americans to travel.*
>
> *These carriages have another advantage, they keep up the idea of equality. The member of Congress is placed by the side of the shoemaker who elected him; they fraternize together and converse with familiarity. You see no person here taking upon himself those important airs, which you often meet with in France. In that country, a man of condition would blush to travel in a diligence, it is an ignoble carriage; one knows not with whom he may find himself. Besides, it is in style to "run post"; this style serves to humiliate those who are condemned to a sad mediocrity.*

What was de Warville doing in America in 1788? He considered himself an abolitionist, finding France's slave colonies to be anathema to his revolutionary philosophy. So he was on a journey to meet up with American abolitionists. Thomas Jefferson noted that de Warville thought well enough of America to consider immigrating there with his wife and children before he and his party were caught up in the early flames of revolution, becoming members of the National Assembly.

Soon alarmed by extreme revolutionary reactions, including the execution of the king, de Warville and his faction proposed more moderate steps, such as promoting a constitutional monarchy. This did not go over well with the Montagnards or the Sans Culottes in the National Guard. They called for the Girondins' removal and arrest from the convention in May 1793. At first, the assembly refused.

The National Guard surrounded the convention meeting with cannons, threatening to blast the entire gathering if the Girondins were not handed over for arrest. The assembly took another vote and complied. Although he escaped briefly, de Warville was soon apprehended. Accused by Robespierre and Marat of spying and other crimes of disloyalty, the Girondins were sentenced to death by guillotine on October 30. The next day, he and his fellows were taken to the point of execution by tumbrel—a lowly two-wheeled cart—singing the revolutionary anthem "La Marseillaise" on the way to their deaths.

AN ENGLISHMAN IS UNIMPRESSED

Businessman Charles W. Janson was less impressed by the possibilities of fresh air and found the particulars of his experience wryly amusing. Neither was he impressed by the free association between the rabble and their betters.

> *I now mounted for the first time, an American Stage, literally a kind of Light Waggon. While I attempt to describe this clumsy and uncomfortable machine, I cannot suppress the wish to being possessed of one of them, with horses, harness, and driver, just as we set off in order to convert them into an exhibition in London.*
>
> *This vehicle which is on the same construction throughout the country is calculated to hold twelve persons, who all sit on benches placed across, with their faces toward the horses. The front seat holds three, one of whom is the driver, and as there are no doors at the sides, the passengers get in over the front wheels, and take their seats as they enter; the first, of course, gets seats behind the rest. This is the most esteemed seat because you can rest your shaken frame against the back part of the waggon.*
>
> *Women are therefore generally indulged with it, and it is often laughable to see them crawling to their seats; and if they happen to be late, they have to straddle over the men who are seated farther in front. It is covered with leather, and instead of windows there are flaps of that article, which in bad weather are let down, and secured by buckles and straps. In summer these flaps are folded up, and this is some alleviation from the repeated shocks you receive in going over the roads, many of which are never repaired.*

As his diary from 1793 to 1806 reveals, despite spending some years in its hinterlands, Janson did not take to America or its "rabble" that did not know their place. Neither did America take to Janson, who eventually returned to his home country after several failed business ventures.

Although Janson mocked the lack of doors on the "light waggon," some did have them—and early on, too. *Stage Coaches and Waggons* quotes a 1764 advertisement from a Philadelphia coachmaker for "A compleat, neat new Waggon, ornamented with Brass Nails, finished after the fashion of a coach, with the Door in the side thereof and leather curtains all round, except in the front, also a neat Coach Harness for a Pair of Horses."

Perhaps Janson was particularly unlucky in his travel adventures—that, or the American rabble did not cotton to his attitude and treated him accordingly.

IV
TOWN TO TOWN

FAYETTE PUDDING

SLICE a loaf of bread tolerably thick—lay the slices in the bottom of a dish, cutting them so as to cover it completely; sprinkle some sugar and nutmeg, with a little butter, on each layer; when all are in, pour on a quart of good boiled custard sweetened—serve it up cold.

A KNACK FOR ORGANIZATION

As the French and Indian War trained up a generation of colonials in how to fight a long-term engagement, in the aftermath of the Revolution, it became evident that the organizational abilities that were necessary—and polished—by years of moving troops and supplies to the battlegrounds and organizing swift riders to carry messengers would come into play again as the young republic set up lines of communication between its citizens.

George Weedon and Levi Pease were certainly excellent examples of that. Weedon would serve as an official local postmaster, and Pease's ability to manage a viable transportation system while limiting corruption by not having individual drivers handle ticket sales made them obvious choices for the trust of public duties. Other veterans would also translate their wartime experiences into practical careers.

Nathanel Twining, late of the Fourth Maryland Regiment and later yet a tavern keeper on the banks of the Susquehanna, started a stage line running between Baltimore and Annapolis three times a week in 1793. Twining partnered with Gabriel Van Horn, who had run a line of express riders during the war. Now a tavern keeper, too, but in Baltimore, Van Horn received a commission from the Maryland legislature in 1785 to run stage lines exclusively from the Susquehanna to the Potomac.

In 1784, Twining was given exclusive rights by the Virginia legislature to run a stage line between Alexandria and Richmond within a year after having successfully opened a line between Baltimore and Alexandria.

The act also allowed Twining to charge passengers "five pence per mile, and five pence per mile for every one hundred and fifty pounds weight of baggage."

IT'S WHOM YOU KNOW

Twining had his important connections, including Henry Lee, who conveyed in a 1788 letter to future president James Madison that he was writing in support of Twining, who had not been paid for his mail runs by Postmaster General Ebenezer Hazard despite having been promised he would. Hazard did have his virtues and his supporters. John Adams considered Hazard a genius, particularly impressed by his desire to save and reprint historic documents so they would not be lost to future generations.

Twining's associate in Virginia was Colonel John Hoomes, who was given the exclusive right to transport persons between Richmond and Petersburg and between Petersburg and Norfolk and Portsmouth.

Colonel Hoomes lived in Bowling Green (Caroline County, Virginia), where he ran a tavern and kept a racetrack. Hoomes bred and raced fine Thoroughbreds—a common passion of the Virginia gentry. He owned Diomed, a national favorite, and sold Thomas Jefferson his fine bay horse Wildair. Colonel Hoomes lived with his family at Old Mansion—still in existence today—and kept his New Hope Tavern at the intersection of the stage road and the rolling road used to get tobacco down to the river at Port Royal.

The Richmond-to-Petersburg route, formerly granted to Richard Towns and John Woolfolk (a friend of Colonel Hoomes), was awarded to William Pennock in 1789. Pennock would later have a grand house designed by Benjamin Henry Latrobe, famous architect and surveyor of public buildings for Thomas Jefferson. Latrobe would have some wry observations on tavern accommodations, which are noted later in this chapter.

BY COACH AND BY BOAT

In 1789, Joseph Wilsey of North Carolina, James Rosekrans of New York, and Robert Twiford of Accomack were granted the exclusive privilege of running a stage waggon from Northampton Courthouse to the line of Maryland. They were also awarded the right to establish one or more packet boats for the purpose of conveying their stage passengers across the Chesapeake Bay from the Eastern Shore to the towns of Norfolk and Portsmouth. Rates for the packet boat trips were established at fifteen shillings per passenger and fifteen shillings for each horse.

Of course, there were taverns and inns along the way to meet the needs of travelers. Dating to about 1780, historic Eastville Inn's prime bay location in Cape Charles has inspired many chefs. It was later known as Taylor House. In recent years, it has been used as a restaurant and catering site. An 1879 write-up described the area as a kind of paradise: "The waters team with oyster, fish, terrapin, and crabs, the long stretches of marshy shore the wild fowl." The accompanying illustration shows an African American woman ringing the "Dinner-bell at an Eastville Tavern," whose sign reads Taylor House, J.A. Jarvis, proprietor.

As Holmes writes, by the end of 1784, stages were running a long distance below Baltimore and Annapolis. From Richmond, Virginia, there

Left: Eastville Inn, Eastville, Northampton County, Virginia, 1934. *Photograph by Frances Benjamin Johnston, courtesy of the Carnegie Survey of the Architecture of the South, Library of Congress.*

Right: "Dinner-bell at an Eastville Tavern," 1870s. *From* Harper's Magazine, *New York Public Library Digital Collections.*

was now an unbroken line of communication to the northern cities, even to Boston, because the gap between New York and Boston was closed in the autumn of the same year. Indeed, Talmadge Hall, tavern keeper of Norwalk (Connecticut) Hall, advertised in the *New-York Packet* "that he had erected a genteel stage waggon with four good Horses, in order to convey ladies and gentlemen and their baggage, in one day and a half, from New York to Stratford Ferry, 74 miles, which compleats the whole line from Richmond in Virginia to Boston as there are stage wagons erected on every other part of the road."

A TALENTED SCAPEGRACE

Stage drivers, who might have to face extreme obstacles in their duties, were accustomed to independence and looking out for themselves, so much so that, as *Stagecoach East* relates, "One Stavers some years ago began to drive a stage coach between Portsmouth and Boston, his drivers hurt the office very much by carrying letters, and they were so artful that the postmaster cou'd not detect them; it was therefore judged proper to take this man into the pay of the office."

So Stavers was rewarded for his bit of chicanery, being paid ten pounds annually for his now official efforts. Other drivers simply carried the mail unofficially with unrepentant spirits. As the postmaster of Salem noted: "the drivers take many letters so that but few are forwarded by Post," adding "an informer wou'd get tar'd and feathere'd."

Having stagecoaches unofficially carry letters as a matter of personal contract was common practice after the Revolution, but it went against the Post Office Ordinance of 1782, which specified that the postmaster general, his deputies and agents, "and no other person whatsoever, shall have the receiving, taking up, ordering, dispatching, sending post or with speed, carrying and delivering of any letters, packets or other despatches from any place within these United States for hire, reward, or other profit or advantage."

THE SPORTING SCENE

Benjamin Henry Latrobe. *Portrait by Filippo Costaggini, courtesy of the Architect of the Capitol.*

Taverns were very much an established part of these communities, and it was in the state's best interest that they be run well. According to *America's Early Taverns*, tavern owners who did not adhere to the conditions of their licenses or violated community standards could lose those licenses. In a small community, a tavern might be expected to do double duty as a church on Sunday if there were no other building available.

Then there were the communities where standards were rather more a matter of a sporting proposition. Great interest in horse racing continued to be tied to taverns in the decades following the Revolution. In Dinwiddie County below Richmond, taverns remained part of the sporting scene, with cockfights and card-playing rounding out the entertainment. Architect Benjamin Henry Latrobe wrote in his diary on April 21, 1796:

> *The case is desperate in a house occupied by seventy men in leather breeches. I rode yesterday to see the race, accompanied by Mr. Thomas Shore.... The accommodations at Mrs. Armistead's are quite as good as you ought to expect at such a time as this. I slept in a garret with seven other gentlemen.... They snored so I couldn't sleep. The concourse upon the race mound was very great indeed—perhaps fifteen hundred persons.*

There were at least three race courses adjacent to Petersburg. Famous horses that ran in those days before and after the Revolution included Janus (a foundation sire for the Quarter Horse breed), Tattersall's Highflyer, Coeur-de-Lion, Rattler, Childers and Timoleon. Famous horsemen of the time who attended included John Randolph of Roanoke and Colonel William Ransom Johnson, "the Napoleon of the Turf."

Sir Archy, a Virginia-bred Thoroughbred, was considered to be one of the best racehorses of his time, and his name can be found in the pedigrees of many winning racehorses today. Foaled in 1805, he passed through several hands before being acquired by Colonel Johnson, who also trained him. In

Sir Archy, famous American Thoroughbred stallion. *From Frank Forester,* Horse and Horsemanship of the United States, vol. 1, *1857.*

Pride's Tavern, Dinwiddie County, Virginia, 1933. *Photograph by Frances Benjamin Johnston, courtesy of the Carnegie Survey of the Architecture of the South, Library of Congress.*

those days, racehorses were expected to run at least two and possibly as many as four four-mile heats for one race, so stamina was a prime factor. Sir Archy won the Jockey Club Purse at Petersburg in 1809 before being retired to stud in North Carolina. He was inducted into the U.S. Racing Hall of Fame in 1955. Readers with a strong interest in horse racing during this period may wish to consult another book by the author, *Virginia Horse Racing: Triumphs of the Turf* (The History Press, 2008).

Both Pride's Tavern (with its adjacent Pride's Race Track) and Bromley's Tavern (home of the Petersburg Jockey Club) were gathering sites for "turfmen," as they styled themselves. During race weeks, all of the neighborhood gentry who did not oppose racing and its related merriment on religious or moral grounds might be found entertaining and being entertained.

POINTS WEST

Rather different scenarios played out at small communities and taverns in the western parts of the state during the eighteenth century. The Tidewater region had almost a 120-year jump on the Shenandoah Valley for settlement. When the valley first opened to European colonists in great numbers in the 1730s, these largely German, Scots-Irish, Swiss and French families traveled down the Great Valley Road with an eye to starting farms and beginning communities. That road, once a warriors' path and hunting trail, followed the sturdy limestone ridges that can be found throughout the area. Land speculators, such as Jost Hite, James Patton and William Beverley, and land companies, often financed by Tidewater families, were major proponents.

ROADS IN THE MOUNTAINS

This wilderness was not tamed, and its native inhabitants were neither friendly nor pacified. Pioneers required physical and emotional strength to survive it. Some of the tribes were friendly with the French, so the French and Indian War played out among these peripheral settlements.

Again, the first roads followed existing trails. Civilization might consist of a fort, and, later on, small communities would spring up around mills, churches and blacksmith's shops. The everyday inns that were built in the shadow of the mountains and along their slopes catered to these pioneer spirits. Unlike the tidewaters leading up to the rivers' fall lines, waterways were seldom an option for travel.

The old Three Notch'd Road led from Staunton to Richmond, but much trade happened along the line of the Great Waggon Road. This byway followed the Shenandoah Valley up to Philadelphia, which is where many immigrants had entered the colonies. Most of the trade followed the same road, which meant that the produce of the fertile valley farms would bypass Virginia's markets and port towns.

In 1748, advocates for trade with Virginia's eastern counties were able to secure funding for a nonmilitary road leading from Pignut Mountain (in today's Fauquier County) to the Blue Ridge at Ashby's Gap. Quickly, funding followed to improve Blue Ridge crossings at Swift Run Gap (today's Route 33 in Greene County) and at Wood's (Jarman's) Gap, where Three Notch'd Road ran from Albemarle County into the Shenandoah Valley.

THE FRENCH AND INDIAN WAR

British general Edward Braddock was defeated by the French near Fort Duquesne, where the Allegheny and Monongahela Rivers joined, in 1755. This area would later be developed as Pittsburgh. As a result, open warfare with hostile Indian tribes broke out all along the western frontier. This led to the British building forts along the Allegheny Mountains near what is now West Virginia. These new forts had to be supplied, which meant better roads had to be built to ensure their security. Even with roads being made to the west, what kinds of taverns and inns could you expect in a territory where most citizens thought it prudent to keep their guns handy and their powder dry? Reports on their hospitality varied.

Captain John Ashby served as a scout in the French and Indian War, and he opened an ordinary (tavern) on the Shenandoah River. John Ashby and his successor in the ordinary trade, Joseph Berry, operated a ferry across the river. Young George Washington recorded spending a night there while working as a surveyor on March 12, 1747/8. At Captain Ashby's, according to his journal, "Nothing remarkable happen'd."

The same could not be said for his lodgings on March 15, when he stayed at Penningtons.

> *We got our suppers & was Lighted into a Room & I not being so good a woodsman as ye rest of my company, striped myself very orderly and went into ye Bed, as they calld it, when to my surprize, I found it to be nothing but a little straw matted together without sheets or any thing else, but only one thread bear blanket with double its weight of vermin, such as Lice, Fleas, &c. I was glad to get up (as soon as ye Light was carried from us.) I put on my cloths & lay as my companions. Had we not been very tired, I am sure we should not have slep'd much that night. I made a Promise not to sleep so from that time forward, chusing rather to sleep in ye open air before a fire, as will appear hereafter.*

Fortunately, the next night brought the survey crew to a much better resting place.

> *We set out early & finish'd about one o'clock & then Travelled up to Frederick Town, where our Baggage came to us. We cleaned ourselves (to get Rid of ye Game we had catched ye night before). I took a Review of ye Town & then return'd to our Lodgings where we had a good Dinner prepared for us. Wine & Rum Punch in plenty, & a good Feather Bed with clean sheets, which was a very agreeable regale.*

It is little wonder that wise travelers brought their own bedclothes, not knowing where they might be expected to rest their heads.

ALONG WINCHESTER ROAD

Farther east, there is a still-standing building that saw a lot of use from travelers during the colonial period and into the nineteenth century, and it went by many names. Today it is sometimes called Yew Hill–Robert Ashby's Tavern–Shacklett's Tavern. It is located on private land near Delaplane (Piedmont Station) in Fauquier County, facing east towards what is now Route 17 but was once better known as Winchester Road—a major thoroughfare between the Shenandoah farming country and the Tidewater area. Today it is an active cattle farm.

Winchester still has several buildings that served as taverns during the stagecoaches' prime seasons. Red Lion Tavern on Loudoun Street was built by Peter Lauck about 1783. Lauck was a member of Morgan's Rifles who fought with George Washington. Severely wounded by a cannon discharge during the Battle of Quebec, his eardrums burst, and he was deaf for the rest of his life.

Old Taylor Hotel in Winchester was built by Bushrod Taylor in 1848 on the site of McGuire Tavern, which dated back to before the American Revolution and was destroyed by a fire. Old Taylor Hotel was a stagecoach stop and post office from at least 1850. It was used as General "Stonewall" Jackson's first headquarters when he commanded the Valley District and later would house wounded soldiers. After undergoing a number of identity changes in the twentieth century (theater, department store and telecom center), it fell into total disuse. It was in such bad shape that it was nearly razed, but the City of Winchester decided to save it. It now houses five apartments and has a two-level restaurant space. In the process of renovation, the old additions were taken down, and that area was turned into a pocket park with a pavilion.

ON THE WAY TO MONTICELLO

The Gordon Inn (also known as Gordon's Tavern) at Gordonsville was, unsurprisingly, built by a Gordon—Nathaniel Gordon—in 1787, just in time to take advantage of the increase in stagecoach lines. This was a popular place for dignitaries in the area, including George Washington, James Madison (who lived a mere nine miles away at Montpelier), James Monroe and many others. The tavern was a noted stagecoach stop at

The Exchange Hotel in Gordonsville. *Photograph by Rutke421, from Wikimedia Commons.*

the junction of two roads, one that led to Fredericksburg and one that led to Richmond.

It was an excellent location and apparently well run. Indeed, President Jefferson approved and recommended Gordon's in an 1802 letter to his daughter as a "good tavern." Gordon's Tavern had a long and lively life, but it was demolished in 1947. It stood approximately at the point where the traffic circle is now. Visitors can still get a view of what is believed to be the tavern's old stables (built around 1805) on the corner of Gentry Drive and East Gordon Avenue. These have been remodeled into a private residence.

What you can see in Gordonsville is the Exchange Hotel, located adjacent to the railroad tracks. This small and lovely museum has a lot of history. It was originally built by Richard Omohundro to take advantage of the new railroad lines running through the town by the 1840s. It burned right before the Civil War but was rebuilt in good style just in time to play an important role as a hospital for wounded troops, and that history is included as part of the museum's exhibits. It is also considered an African American heritage site, as it was used from the time after the war through the 1880s as a Freedman's Bureau, offering schooling and court services for former slaves.

The second-story porch at the Exchange Hotel. *Author's photograph.*

Gordonsville was dubbed "the Chicken Leg Capital of the Universe" by a newspaperman named Bagby who noted the enterprising families, mainly African American, who would meet the trains with baskets of fried chicken to sell to hungry passengers. The town revives that tradition on special occasions, but you can always enjoy another traditional Southern staple at the Barbeque Exchange, right across the tracks from the Exchange Hotel.

MICHIE TAVERN

If nothing will do but colonial history—and fried chicken—you may want to continue on to Michie Tavern, now located on the same mountain as Jefferson's Monticello right outside Charlottesville.

In the 1920s, Michie's Tavern was described by Elise Lathrop in *Early American Inns and Taverns* as "an old inn…practically unchanged, off the beaten track." Its large frame building was then occupied as "cheap apartments" and was "rapidly tumbling to pieces." That observer would not recognize today's Michie Tavern. In a spirit of practicality and preservation, a local businesswoman who purchased the property in 1927 had the entire site moved seventeen miles by horse and wagon and truck from its rusticating setting to a location adjacent to one of the most popular tourist spots in the state. That has proven to be a wise move. Michie's is a tavern that, like the Rising Sun in Fredericksburg, can be toured. It also offers a delicious lunch, with house-fried chicken taking center stage.

Michie's Old Tavern, Charlottesville, Albemarle County, Virginia, 1933. *Photograph by Frances Benjamin Johnston, courtesy of the Carnegie Survey of the Architecture of the South, Library of Congress.*

Michie Tavern was built in the 1780s by another Revolutionary War veteran, William Michie. Michie, like the Jouetts, had signed the Albemarle Declaration of 1779 against the king. The son of "Scotch John" Michie, he had served during the winter at Valley Forge before being summoned home to look after his ailing father. When he was ready, he decided to place his tavern in the shadow of Bucks Mountain, although that would not be its final location. Its new (though nearly a century old now) view also affords visitors a chance to gather apples at adjacent Carter Mountain Orchard or take a tour of Monticello.

In Charlottesville itself, there were many taverns, including the Swan Tavern, owned by Jack Jouett's father, and the post-Revolution Eagle Tavern on Court Square, that are no longer standing.

A WATERING HOLE WITH A NAUGHTY NAME

However, there are some gems remaining. Located about a mile from the University of Virginia, today's Ivy Inn continues a tradition of hospitality. Originally built as a tavern in the early 1700s, it was destroyed by a fire and rebuilt in 1816. It went through several sales during the nineteenth and twentieth centuries. Today, it offers fine dining in an elegant and historic atmosphere. Several of its dishes, such as crab cakes and ham biscuits, would have been familiar to visitors in times past.

A more rustic tavern in the area that has lately been used as a private residence is the D.S. Tavern, located along Three-Notch'd Road to the west of Charlottesville. It was at one time owned by Chief Justice John Marshall.

Early America had its share of jokesters, and one of them surely named the tavern called Pinch-'em-Slyly. Built about 1792 west of Charlottesville's Stonybrook area, its grounds were used by the local Barterbrook militia as a muster point and practice area. The tavern is no longer standing, but the road that led to it still bears the name.

A HANDSOME TAVERN IN PITTSYLVANIA COUNTY

Another tavern built to welcome western travelers survives to this day. Yates Tavern is a fully restored eighteenth-century building with a true pioneer feel to it, and it is listed in the National Register of Historic Places. In recent years, local historians have held reenactments focused on its colonial past. Built around 1750, the house is made from weatherboarding and has a rock chimney. There is a large public room with a rock fireplace beneath an impressive mantel. A smaller adjoining main-floor room has a closet under the staircase. The corner stairway leads to a two-roomed loft upstairs.

The English basement, half in and half out of the ground, has walls two feet thick, the better to protect against possible attacks. Meals were prepared in the enormous basement fireplace. There is trapdoor access from the main floor into the basement. Yates Tavern is open by appointment through the Pittsylvania Historical Society.

MEANWHILE, IN SOUTH CENTRAL VIRGINIA…

Old Boyd Tavern is a national landmark in Boydton. Like Gordonsville, the town was named for one of its leading citizens who also happened to run a thriving tavern business.

Boyd's Tavern, constructed in 1785, was also known as Boydton Hotel and the Exchange Hotel. It was originally licensed by Richard Swepson Jr., who ran it until he chose to sell it to his brother-in-law, Alexander Boyd. Like Gordonsville's Exchange Hotel, it now has a two-story porch, added during one of its several renovations. Boyd's provided overnight accommodations near the courthouse (and the stocks…and the jail). The rise in popularity of the stagecoach was good for business at Boyd's. The tavern served as a stagecoach depot, as it lay along a road connecting the town with Petersburg, and it catered to clientele of rather the higher classes.

According to BoydTavern.net: "In 1811, Alexander Boyd described his establishment as having, 'a table amply supplied with all the meat raised in this part of the Country and a cellar furnished with the liquors of Europe, Africa and America; a tavern with fourteen rooms and twelve fireplaces… with stables as good as any in the state.'"

Later owner William Townes expanded the premises to include a racetrack. It already had a storehouse, stables and shoe shop. These extras have faded away, but the tavern has seen much use through the centuries.

Boydton, nicknamed "the Town That Refused to Die," has developed a very nice historic district that features the tavern, with more than two hundred structures contributing to the district. Boydton Historic District was added to the National Register of Historic Places in 2002. Its tavern is open for tours on weekdays, but call ahead to check its current hours. There are regular celebrations at Boydton, including Boydton Day, a relatively new tradition (1977) with parades, speeches, food and music every October.

CHARMING MIDDLEBURG HAS SEEN MUCH HISTORY

Tiny Middleburg, Virginia, is surrounded by fields groomed for foxhunting, and it is truly one of the most equine-centric parts of the state. Today's visitors can enjoy visiting the National Sporting Library & Museum and spend hours poring over accounts of the Old Dominion's history with horses and hounds.

One of the favorite places for hospitality among eighteenth-century countrymen—and women—was Chinn's Crossroads, and its strong walls were a place of refuge during the American Revolution. Established in 1728, the inn was expanded about 1812 to include a large wine cellar and changed its name to the Beverage House. It was a military headquarters and hospital during "the Late Unpleasantness"—a more local name for the Civil War. Today, the shingle hanging outside the door reads the Red Fox Inn, a most appropriate name, as Middleburg is the seat of much horse and hound activity. Visitors can still enjoy a sumptuous meal or take a room at this remarkable Loudoun County inn.

BIDE A WHILE AT THE WAYSIDE INN

In Middletown, Virginia, the Wayside Inn has been offering hospitality to travelers to the Shenandoah Valley since 1797. Originally known as

Wilkenson's Tavern, it became more popular when the Valley Pike (today's Route 11) passed through Middletown. It was a popular stagecoach stop. According to the inn:

> *In coaching days, a servant boy would be sent to the nearby hill to sight an expected stagecoach. When a cloud of dust appeared over the horizon, he waited anxiously, straining to sight the outline of the stagecoach, and then hurried back to the Inn to report its approach. By the time the passengers arrived, delicious hot food would be waiting and they would dine and drink in comfort while the team of horses was being changed.*

Before the Civil War, it was bought by Jacob Larrick, who changed the name to Larrick's Hotel. It gained its current name in the early part of the twentieth century when new owner Samuel Rhodes expanded it by adding a third floor and wings to either side.

It was purchased in the 1960s by financier Leo M. Bernstein, who restored it and refurbished it with antiques. This old and storied tavern and inn with twenty-two rooms is still welcoming guests, including wedding parties.

THE NATIONAL ROAD

In 1818, the federal government's first major road project came to fruition, as it connected Cumberland, Maryland, with Wheeling, (West) Virginia, on the Ohio River. The National Road (also known as the Cumberland Road) had been an idea of both Washington's and Jefferson's to bind the eastern states with the western ones.

A team of Friesians at the Morven Park Carriage Show. *Author's photograph.*

Virginia by Stagecoach

Top: The First National Road, begun in 1811. *U.S. Post Office, author's collection.*

Bottom: Old Stone Tavern, Route 50, New Creek, Mineral County, West Virginia, 1933. *Courtesy of the Historic American Buildings Survey, Library of Congress.*

In part, it followed an old trail called Nemacolin's Path that ran from the Potomac to the Ohio River. That route had long been used by traders. It joined with another road that ran from Baltimore to Boonesboro.

Nemacolin (ca. 1715–ca. 1767) was a chief of the Delaware. He, along with English colonel Thomas Cresap (who later had an inter-colony war named after him), widened the path to the Ohio Valley from 1748 to 1750 so that freight wagons could navigate it. A little later on, George Washington and his troops would do some more road work to aid British general Braddock's ill-fated expedition.

Near Cumberland in Frostburg, Maryland, visitors can see many kinds of horse-drawn vehicles at the Thrasher Carriage Museum, which also has resources for people who are interested in taking up the old skills of carriage driving. There is another carriage museum at Morven Park near Leesburg, Virginia. Morven Park hosts carriage competitions that can give viewers a taste of days gone by.

By the late 1820s, the Old Northwest Turnpike connected Winchester, Virginia, to the Ohio River at Parkersburg. Handsome Old Stone Tavern, in Mineral County, West Virginia, was built about 1810. Also known as Old Stone House or Traveler's Rest, it is about a mile east of Ridgeville on U.S. 50 (Route 50 was once the Northwest Turnpike) in Burlington, West Virginia. Traveler's Rest served as a stagecoach stop. Today, it is a gathering spot for special events in the community, and money is being raised to complete its restoration.

Since the time of the old picture in the Library of Congress's building survey, its porch and greenery have been removed, as has one chimney. It has survived into the twenty-first century and is now owned by the Mineral County Historical Foundation and is listed in the National Register of Historic Places.

HISTORY UNEARTHED IN CENTREVILLE

Newgate Tavern once stood at the intersection of what are now Route 28 and Route 29 in Centreville, an area once known as Newgate. It was opened about 1768 by William Carr Lane, whose family also sold convicted servants—which may be related to its name, as Newgate was a famous prison in England. Newgate Tavern, also known as Lane's Ordinary, was a popular stop along the way to Northwest Territory. George Washington was reported to have visited it on at least four occasions. In its heyday, there were local horse races

Newgate Tavern, Centreville, Fairfax County, Virginia, 1933. *Courtesy of the Historic American Buildings Survey, Library of Congress.*

sponsored by the Centreville Jockey Club, and the tavern also hosted balls. By the early 1800s, it had been renamed the Eagle Tavern. Although demolished in the 1930s after years of neglect, a subdivision and a shopping center bear its original name, and an archaeological excavation uncovered its remains. In 2013, a marker was placed near its site at 13923 Braddock Road.

PUSHING FARTHER WEST

In time, settlers would cross the Alleghenies, a territory that was then still considered Virginia. The first recorded settlers were Jacob Marlin and Stephen Sewell. In 1749, they settled at present-day Marlinton in Pocahontas County. An argument over religion led them to part company, but not too far, as those were those dangerous days. The story has it that by the time father-and-son surveyors John and Andrew Lewis discovered the men in 1751 at Knapps Creek, Stephen Sewell had moved into a nearby giant (and hollow) sycamore tree. Eventually, they parted company entirely and went on to claim land elsewhere. Sewell Mountain is named for the one man, who died in an Indian attack in 1756, and the town of Marlinton is named for the other.

John and Andrew Lewis were from County Donegal in Ireland. Andrew (1720–1781) became friends with another young surveyor of the time, George Washington. Andrew would go on to be a member of the Virginia House of Burgesses and lead an army of militiamen to defeat tribes led by

Cornstalk at the Battle of Point Pleasant in 1774. Lewisburg, the seat of Greenbrier County, is named for Andrew and his family.

The early route over what would be known as Sewell Mountain was first known, unsurprisingly, as the Lewis Trail. It would later be known as the Midland Trail and lead to West Virginia's eventual capital at Charleston on the Kanawha River. Once numbers were assigned to routes in the twentieth century, it was called Route 60, and until the completion of I-64 in the late 1980s, it was a popular if challenging route across the mountains that can still be driven by the adventurously minded. In earlier days, it was the only choice.

FROZEN IMPERIALS IN THE SHADOW OF PETERS MOUNTAIN

At the junction of Routes 159 and 11 in Alleghany County, Virginia, there's a place called Crows—not named for the birds said to gather in a murder but rather for a Colonel John Crow who operated a tavern here. Colonel Crow, who had served in the Alleghany militia, entertained and boarded people at his tavern. Some were farmers and drovers taking their stock to market. Others were travelers on their way to enjoy the society and presumed health benefits of the nearby springs.

In any event, Colonel Crow was a teller of tales at his Old Crow Tavern, a building made with pegged doors and fireplaces in every one of its approximately seventeen rooms. The kitchen fireplace was in a separate building and was said to be large enough to accommodate logs eight feet long.

Mrs. Adcock, whose family purchased the tavern about 1900, related one of Colonel Crow's stories:

> *He would tell people who stayed over that he once made a bet with a man and said if that fellow started to Covington on his horse, he could be in Covington before* [the other fellow] *got there. Col. Crow had a pet bear, and he got on that bear's back to go across the mountain, and along the way somewhere that old bear saw a female bear and threw him off and took off. He never made it to Covington and never won that bet, either.*

Crow Tavern, Alleghany County, Virginia, 1935. *Photograph by Frances Benjamin Johnston, courtesy of the Carnegie Survey of the Architecture of the South, Library of Congress.*

More is told of the hospitality one might find at Old Crow Tavern and the colonel in the article "Early History of Monroe: James and John Crow":

> *He was known far and wide for the excellent food served as well as for the many wild stories he related. Prices of food varied according to the quantity and the manner served: hot meals were slightly more costly than a cold diet. Both were sold with a small beer. Whiskey was about 5 shillings per gallon. If a traveler wanted a clean bed without a bedfellow he would have to pay 8 ½ cents but if he allowed another guest to share the bed with him, the charges were only 5 ½ cents. Botetourt County (as it was then known) had set the rates a few years earlier at slightly less and added that if more than two persons shared one bed there would be no charge. However, it was unlawful for more than four persons to occupy the bed at the same time. All kinds of beverages were offered in the Tavern: peach brandy, apple brandy, Malt Beer, French Brandy, Bumbo with two gills of rum to the quart made with sugar, and of course, whiskey in quantity to cheer the weary body.*

Virginia by Stagecoach

Mary Hagner of New York, writing under the pen name of Mark Pencil, Esq., had this to say about a visit to Old Crow Tavern:

> *One fine racy morning, before sunrise, throwing our cloaks over our shoulders, we rolled off in an open carriage to make a visit to the Sweet Springs, and enjoy the ride before breakfast. We left White Sulphur long before the inhabitants of Paradise Row were stirring, and in a little while our dapples were winding their way through some of the finest scenery romance or poetry has ever pictured—over a smooth beaten road, which seemed to have been carved through the mountains...*
>
> *A ride of ten miles brought us to Crow's, with a fine relish of breakfast, or anything else that might be offered to us. This is the place where so many excursions are made from the Springs for dinner parties and picnics. The tavern stands on the corner of the road at the foot of a mountain, and the signboard swings out front.*
>
> *We entered the white palings through a wicket gate and were met on the piazza by Mr. Crow, quite portly, and good natured in appearance, somewhat of a politician, besides being a colonel. He promised us all we required, and brought a frozen imperial to refresh us.* [This may be frozen imperial punch, referenced in the December 20, 1891 *Boston Globe*.]
>
> *Colonel Crow has a large garden attached to his establishment, where we gathered a bouquet of jessamines, and went on to the Sweet.*

Another traveler, Captain Page McCarty of Richmond, wrote:

> *The host, Colonel Crow, was a distinct type of his class, a prince withal, whose eccentricities and power of drinking placed him at the top of the calling. He was very red and portly, good-humored and jovial, and owing to a brilliant and cultivated imagination, had attained all over the state of Old Virginia, far and wide, the proud title of "the biggest liar that walked on two legs."*

And, yes, there's more on that bear:

> *Col. Crow had a pet bear named Bruin. There was a special attachment between the pet and master. If Bruin became too rough Col. Crow would chastise him with a long wagon whip. Bruin would retire to the forks of a big oak tree in the yard and wait until he thought his master had "repented*

the punishment" and then come down and stand on his hind legs, it is said, with tears in his eyes, until Colonel Crow made friends with him...

It is also noted that Bruin did, indeed, carry Colonel Crow around on his back.

Upon the colonel's death in 1861, verses in his honor were carved on a nearby sycamore tree:

*Old Crow is dead, that good old soul,
Who used to brew our wassail bowl.
His cheek was red and his nose was blue,
But his hand was strong and his heart was true.
He drank all day and he drank all night.
At last he drank old Satan tight.
For when the devil caught his ghost,
Crow never ceased to call his toast,
Till the devil thought he had caught a Monk,
And staggered back into hell dead drunk,
And Crow skipped aloft like a shooting star,
And asked Saint Peter to show him the bar.*

Unfortunately, Old Crow Tavern burned down in 1970, but the community still has the colonel's name. Presumably, the bears are still in residence, too. Nearby, Peters Mountain Wilderness is managed by Jefferson National Forest.

AT THE COUNTY SEAT IN LEWISBURG...

Another old tavern in the area—and one that is still standing—is the Star Tavern. Now called the North House Museum, this Lewisburg attraction contains collections from the Greenbrier Historical Society (www.greenbrierhistorical.org). Court clerk John A. North built it in 1820 and sold it to James Frazier in 1830. He converted it into Frazier's Star Tavern. Lawyers and other court visitors were frequent guests. It reverted to a residence when Frazier sold it in 1870.

In the 1920s, it became the president's house for Greenbrier College for Women. It was also used for a time by the Lewisburg Seminary and

Conservatory of Music. The building was taken over by the historical society in 1976. In addition to exhibits that begin with the Revolutionary era, the museum has an archives and library that are open for research.

Built in the Federal style, this spacious and ornate brick building is a cut above the workaday taverns usually found. The historical society recently acquired the title to the Blue Sulphur Springs Pavilion, the only surviving building of the Blue Sulphur Springs Resort, dating to 1834. The society also owns the Barracks, a stopping point for stagecoaches and other travelers. Its rough three-story stone and log exterior likely date to the 1780s. It lies along the Seneca Trail Highway about a block from the Midland Trail Scenic Byway (Route 60).

FARTHER ALONG THE MIDLAND TRAIL

Tyree Tavern, located in Ansted (formerly Mountain Cove), Fayette County, West Virginia, was a stagecoach stop on the James River & Kanawha River Turnpike.

Its original portion was built prior to 1810 and was enlarged to accommodate travelers who used it as an inn after the mid-1820s. Famous guests included Daniel Webster, Henry Clay and John Breckenridge, vice president of the United States and later secretary of war for the Confederacy. It was also known as Halfway House. Several notable features can no longer be seen, including stables that were located across the road, an adjacent weaving shed and a grove of giant walnut trees at the rear of the house. During the Civil War, Tyree Tavern became the headquarters of the Chicago Gray Dragoons. A two-story log and frame structure, it was added to the National Register of Historic Places in 1978.

AT THE FALLS OF THE KANAWHA

Finally down the mountain and into the Kanawha River valley, the Stockton Tavern was surely a welcome sight for travelers who had braved the worst of the mountain roads. Now known as the Glen Ferris Inn and still welcoming visitors, this inn's location at the falls of the Kanawha River made it a beautiful place to stop and rest. Although much remodeled in a classical revival style in 1910, the inn itself has been welcoming travelers since 1839, in the early days of the James River & Kanawha Turnpike. The original owner, Aaron Stockton, was the grandson of Richard Stockton, a signer of the Declaration of Independence. Aaron Stockton acquired the property in 1817. He applied for a liquor license in 1839, which is why we have that as a starting date.

Stockton also made it the center of his many enterprises, including farming, timbering, flatboat building and an early run at commercial coal mining. His property was well placed at the falls, as that was the point where the waters of the Kanawha became navigable.

During the early days of the Civil War (July–September 1861), the Stockton Tavern was used as a U.S. Army quartermaster depot. It went through a time, though still owned by the Stockton family, with the moniker of the Hawkins Hotel. It passed out of the family's hands and into those of a series of industrial owners, beginning with Union Carbide in 1920. They were the ones who renamed it the Glen Ferris Inn and often housed their managers and supervisors there. In 1991, it was accepted in the National Register of Historic Places, and in 1996, it went back into private ownership, though it is still welcoming guests.

Today's Glen Ferris Inn (glenferrisinn.com) features fifteen guest rooms, two suites, the Old Stockton Dining Room and the Riverside Dining Room. According to its National Register nomination, among those said to have been entertained in its old dining room were President John Tyler, naturalist John Audubon, President Andrew Jackson, statesman Henry Clay and Senator Thomas H. Benton.

TAKING THE TURNPIKE

Were the early roads in Virginia terrible? Some travelers, such as Charles Dickens, seemed to think so, but in certain well-traveled sections they were due for an improvement. The turnpike, as promoted by stagecoach pioneer Levi Pease and his compatriots, gave a way to get better roads that was practical, particularly for a young and emerging nation. The first major U.S. toll road was built in the 1790s, connecting the port city of Philadelphia with the farmlands of Lancaster County.

At certain points along these turnpike roads, there would be tolls to be paid, often with a long rail, called a pike, placed across the road to block access and ensure payment. The toll money would go to improve the roads and to pay the toll keeper, whose job it was to make sure that none might pass unless they paid their way or had a pass. Toll keepers often lived adjacent to their pikes in tollhouses, some of which survive today.

These turnpikes were frequented by business people, including farmers, and their routes were practical ones, some of which still see high traffic today. Little River Turnpike, star of many an afternoon traffic report, connected the port city of Alexandria with the productive western farmlands in Loudoun County. Though no longer a turnpike, it retains the historic name. Sometimes, the roads would be built by private funds and mainly intended for private use. In that case, ordinary citizens would be asked to pay a fee to travel on the roads.

Lying along Main Street in Fairfax City, the Ratcliffe-Logan-Allison House once operated as a post office and stagecoach stop in the early 1800s. Also commonly referred to as Earp's Ordinary (although the actual Earp's Ordinary may have preceded it), it was built in two sections about 1810 and 1820. In the late eighteenth century, Fairfax County Circuit Court justice Richard Ratcliffe convinced his fellow justices and the Virginia General

Earp's Ordinary, Fairfax City, Fairfax County, Virginia, 1933. *Courtesy of the Historic American Buildings Survey, Library of Congress.*

Assembly to move the county's courthouse from Alexandria to what is now known as Fairfax City but then wasn't much of anything.

It was to be put at a crossroads called Earp's Corner, where Caleb Earp operated his ordinary. The plan went ahead, as the spot was geographically central for the entire huge county, even though Alexandria, the current location, was quite popular, being a busy port city. As it happened, Richard Ratcliffe owned several thousand acres in the area, which would naturally become more valuable if they were in proximity to the courthouse. Construction began on the civic structure about 1799. Ratcliffe built several taverns and tenements while proffering about four acres of land for municipal buildings.

THE ENTERPRISING RICHARD RATCLIFFE

When Little River Turnpike was constructed in 1801, Richard Ratcliffe was on its board and saw to it that it ran by the new courthouse—and his taverns. Soon he built a race field south of the new courthouse. Race fields and taverns and courthouses went together in a big way during both the colonial and federal periods. The Fairfax Court-House Races were overseen by the Fairfax Jockey Club, comprised of gentlemen in the area. The facility itself was overseen by John Maddox, who in 1810 leased one of two taverns from Richard Ratcliffe, as told in very interesting detail by William Page Johnson II, writing for the *Fare Facs Gazette*. Richard Ratcliffe declared: "The course is handsome, equaled by few on the continent, and in good order."

John Maddox was a well-regarded trainer, and under his management, the racetrack flourished. After Maddox left to head the City Racefield in Washington, the surviving Ratcliffe son, Robert, inherited his father's holdings. Things went well for another six years, but a fire in 1831 at the Virginia Hotel, teeming with guests during court session, was the beginning of the end for the Fairfax Court-House Races.

The Little River Turnpike ran to Aldie, where the Little River cuts through the Blue Ridge. The old route ran from Alexandria to Jermantown (near the Fairfax campus of George Mason University), following the path of today's Route 236. From Jermantown, the route followed the path of today's Route 50 to Aldie. The Ashby Gap Turnpike Company later extended the connection west to the crest of the Blue Ridge.

The Fauquier & Alexandria Turnpike began its incorporation proceedings in 1812, but they were not completed until 1824. This turnpike ran from Alexandria to the Fauquier County Courthouse in Warrenton. Funds were raised to build the road through a lottery as well as by selling stock, and many of its records are available for research at the Library of Virginia in Richmond. Gainesville, on Route 29, was once a place for stagecoaches to change horses.

ALEXANDRIA—A PORT CITY

In the 1700s, when the future Washington, D.C., was just a misty, obscure swamp, Alexandria was one of the most prominent port cities on the Eastern Seaboard. Probably the most famous tavern in Northern Virginia today is Gadsby's in Alexandria. It takes its name from John Gadsby, who operated both a tavern and the hotel in adjacent buildings. Persons of prominence who frequented the establishments included the Marquis de Lafayette, Thomas Jefferson, John Adams, James Monroe and George Washington, who attended balls there given in his honor. Gadsby's fell on hard times by the start of the twentieth century, and its fine woodwork was sold to the Metropolitan Museum of Art in 1917 so the museum could preserve it and display it in its American wing.

When Elise Lathrop wrote her book on American taverns in 1926, she lamented that Gadsby's was now merely a shell of its former self. Demolition seemed its likely fate. Inspired by Lathrop, in 1929, American Legion Post 24 became determined to save the tavern. On the eve of the Great Depression, members literally mortgaged their homes to buy it and, with the help of other historically minded organizations, began a slow process of preservation and restoration. The nation's bicentennial in 1976 gave rise to another wave of interest in historic preservation, and Gadsby's was readied for the spotlight again. Now, Gadsby's consists of a museum, which gives tours and hosts special historical lectures, and a restaurant, which recreates a colonial atmosphere, complete with handsome woodwork—though the original is still in New York City.

Of course, only a few taverns survive to the present, especially in bustling cities such as Alexandria. Flounder Tavern, at Sharpskin and Market Square Alleys, was built about 1800 and, as can be seen in early photographs, was soon conjoined with a twin flounder building, making

Left: City Hotel and Gadsby's Inn, Alexandria, Virginia, 1916–17. *Courtesy of the National Photo Company Collection, Library of Congress.*

Below: Flounder Tavern Building, Sharpskin and Market Square Alleys, Alexandria, Virginia, ca. 1933. *Courtesy of the Historic American Buildings Survey, Library of Congress.*

it look more complete. A flounder is a kind of architectural style with windows on only one side and a sharp, flat windowless main wall, rather resembling the flat-sided fish. There is some speculation that it housed Arell's Tavern, a favorite of George Washington and his fellows. Most of the old buildings in the Market Square were demolished during the city's urban renewal phase in the 1960s, and Flounder Tavern is no more.

WESTWARD, HO!

The Stagecoach Inn, which lay along the Fauquier & Alexandria Turnpike in Buckland (Prince William County), is no longer standing. But the recently opened Buckland Heritage Museum, located in the old "tack shack" at the southeast corner of Lee Highway/U.S. 29 and Vint Hill Road, is on the site of the former stagecoach toll booth stop, and a walking tour brochure of the historic town can be found on the state tourism website.

Following the path of today's Route 29, the Fauquier & Alexandria Turnpike had six toll gates at five-mile intervals. The Stone Bridge and the Stone House, still visible and in good repair on the Manassas Battlefield,

Stone House Tavern, Manassas, Virginia. *Photograph by Carol G. Highsmith, courtesy of the Library of Congress.*

were part of the turnpike, giving farmers between Bull Run and the Rappahannock a way to trade.

The Blue Ridge Turnpike cut Madison County in half, connecting Gordonsville to Sperryville. The Newmarket and Sperryville Pike crossed the Blue Ridge at Thornton Gap.

Farther south and west, the James River & Kanawha Turnpike was completed in the early 1800s. It was the first major east–west route running through what is now southern West Virginia, eventually leading to Richmond. Route 60 over the mountains follows roughly the same path, also known as the Midland Trail. Once a major route to get from Lexington, Virginia, and Greenbrier County, West Virginia, to the capital city of Charleston, Route 60 is now frequently bypassed by travelers who take the much less adventurous Interstate 64 all the way from Charleston, West Virginia, to Richmond. However, a new kind of visitor braves Route 60 to enjoy white water rafting and restful stays at Hawks Nest State Park.

EVER HEARD OF THE NORTHWEST INDIAN WAR?

A journey through these western reaches was not always so peaceful. During the 1780s and 1790s, there was a now mostly forgotten war going on in the "Old Northwest" that followed on the heels of the American Revolution. Ohio would officially be made a state in 1803, but before then, part of it was considered the Virginia Military District and was used as a source of land to reward veterans of the American Revolution, so Virginia very much had an interest in it.

The Northwest Indian War (1785–95), also known as the Ohio War and Little Turtle's War, was an extremely bloody conflict that included one of the Indians' largest victories against the settlers, drawing cooperation from tribes as far away as the Potawatomi of eastern Michigan.

Chief Little Turtle of the Miami, before 1900. *Courtesy of the U.S. Army.*

These Indian tribes, with British backing, continued to struggle for control of the western reaches—although, according to the Treaty of Paris (1783), the British were not supposed to be a presence there any longer. But they elected to keep their forts there, supporting the Indians—who at that time numbered around 45,000—in their drives to force out settlers, prompting President Washington to send in the newly minted U.S. Army, which included many militiamen.

THE LEGION OF THE UNITED STATES

After the Harmar Campaign (1790) and St. Clair's Defeat (1791), also known as the Battle of a Thousand Slain, which were disastrous for the United States, Washington ordered in Revolutionary War hero General "Mad Anthony" Wayne to train and lead the army, which was now dubbed the Legion of the United States, in late 1793.

Now well-led and well-trained, the legion fared far better in the last conflict in the war. The Battle of Fallen Timbers happened on August 20, 1794, near what is now Toledo, Ohio. U.S. troops defeated a confederation of Indians led by Chief Blue Jacket of the Shawnees, Chief Little Turtle of the Miamis and Chief Buckongahelas of the Lenapes. A year after that battle, the Treaty of Greenville opened up what we now call Ohio to settlers.

It was not until these areas were more or less free from attack that European-style inroads could be made to the Ohio and Kanawha Rivers—water routes that would be main arteries for travel and shipping. Stagecoaches would naturally connect settlements farther from the river, and turnpikes would eventually make for better journeys.

A PIECE OF THE PAST

Along Main Street in Barboursville, West Virginia, there is an 1837 log tollhouse that was refurbished by the local D.A.R. chapter in 1950. The building originally stood by the Guyan River. Its staff took tolls from travelers disembarking the ferry on the James River & Kanawha canal-road turnpike, but it fell out of use when a bridge was built to span the river.

The old tollhouse in Barboursville, West Virginia. *Photograph by Carol G. Highsmith, courtesy of the Library of Congress.*

Today, turnpikes are by no means passé, although they no longer feature actual pikes or resident toll keepers. Toll lanes are still quite popular with state budget offices if not with drivers, with thousands of miles of toll roads still generating income.

V
A NIGHT AT A COACHING INN

TAVERN BISCUIT

To one pound of flour, add half a pound of sugar, half a pound of butter, some mace and nutmeg powdered, and a glass of brandy or wine; wet it, with milk, and when well kneaded, roll it thin, cut it in shapes, and bake it quickly.

lthough many did travel from town to town as a matter of business or leisure, a night at a coaching inn might run the gamut from plain and quietly civilized to watering holes for local sportsmen of nearly all social persuasions. While special rooms might be set aside for genteel travelers to enjoy on their own, a traveler with lighter pockets might find himself snug in a bed with several other sojourners, side by side, or perhaps enjoying a pallet of straw of uncertain age upon the bedroom floor.

TO EACH HIS OWN

As noted in Lathrop's *Early American Inns and Taverns*, many public ordinaries in Virginia were not built for permanence, as travelers, even strangers, were often entertained in private homes. Those who stayed overnight in many ordinaries' accommodations tended to be of "the humbler class of traveler who could be comfortable in them."

Because of the uneven quality of accommodations, travelers who could packed their own bed linens, as any number of small pests might be in close attendance after the last candle was extinguished. Those pests frequently included mice or rats as a matter of course, and the better sort of taverns would be well-stocked with lethal and loud mousetraps, as can still be seen at the Rising Sun Tavern in Fredericksburg.

A better sort of room for conviviality might be kept for the gentry and also used for occasional dances. There, some favorite drinks were wines served warm and mulled with spices, as well as punches that might combine milk or cream and strong spirits poured into a large bowl that could be drunk from a shared dipper. Over in the more common taproom, locals might chew what they cut from the gratis plugs of tobacco, enjoy salty snacks and raise their sometimes glass-bottomed tankards in a toast before the firelight. Others preferred to smoke their tobacco, and they would be handed what would start out as a long clay pipe, smoke their fill, break off their used part of the stem, pay for that and hand it along to the next person.

There might be many kinds of entertainment going on in a tavern to appeal to different audiences. The gentry's room might host rather formal dances or gentlemanly card games. A game called faro was quite popular,

Tavern, store and kitchen, Route 29 and Route 631, Madison, Madison County, Virginia, 1933. *Photograph by Louis Nelson, courtesy of the Historic American Buildings Survey, Library of Congress.*

Right: Madison Tavern, staircase, 1933. *Photograph by Louis Nelson, courtesy of the Historic American Buildings Survey, Library of Congress.*

Below: Madison Tavern, second-floor bedroom, 1933. *Photograph by Louis Nelson, courtesy of the Historic American Buildings Survey, Library of Congress.*

Madison Tavern, first floor, 1933. *Photograph by Louis Nelson, courtesy of the Historic American Buildings Survey, Library of Congress.*

with each gambler bringing his or her own chits, some made of mother of pearl. At a ball, quite a lot of courting might go on, as evidenced by Jefferson's Apollo Room diary entry.

    Meanwhile, over in the taproom, there could be music and dancing as well, but it was boisterous, and the taproom guests would enjoy other entertainments such as small circuses and freak shows. In Fredericksburg during the 1800s, the Traveller's Rest (on the south corner of Caroline and Frederick Streets but no longer standing) was the place to find circuses and menageries. It was also a place where regular laboring men came after a day's work and where politicians might ply their craft. Nineteenth-century historian S.J. Quinn called it "a tavern of considerable notoriety and popularity."

FIGHTING WORDS

As will happen when liquor is a lubricant to men's tongues and brains, fights might break out on either side of the tavern as harsh words became hard blows or, in the case of the gentlemen, a cause for a duel. Dueling was extremely common in the South during the antebellum period.

To keep things at some level of civility, most followed a set of rules called a code duello. Interestingly, the rules of a code duello were designed to keep the body count as low as possible. First, the would-be duelists had to go through the formalities of trying to solve their problems without violence. If that failed, the rules of combat limited their opportunity for deadly conflict and ensured that medical help (such as it was in the days before antiseptics) would be on hand. The Irish Code Duello, which came about in the last quarter of the eighteenth century, was also popular in America and consisted of twenty-five rules, including giving choice of weapons to the challenged party.

Today, many American museums that touch on eighteenth- and nineteenth-century life will display braces of dueling pistols from their collections. These were considered by many—including fiery politicians—an essential accessory for a gentleman's kit. What might provoke a duel? A charge of cowardice, for one thing. Naturally, not showing up for a duel was considered proof of cowardice.

One frequent visitor at the Indian Queen Tavern in Fredericksburg was known for his irascible temperament. John Randolph of Roanoke had served as a senator for Virginia. As noted in an article on Fredericksburg hotels by Barbara Crookshanks, he was known for his "elegant, sarcastic, and eccentric" personality and was quick to speak his mind. A group of Democrats asked him to share a communal punch bowl with them. He was not amused: He replied: "I don't drink with strangers and if I can't rest here one night without being disturbed by a mob, I will drive to the Sycamores [an inn on the Bowling Green Road]."

"LIKE A ROTTEN MACKEREL BY MOONLIGHT"

John Randolph was an enthusiastic horseman and part of the dueling culture. In 1826, he and Secretary of State Henry Clay fought a duel on the banks of the Potomac River. The cause was a harangue Randolph

John Randolph. *From an original work by Alonzo Chappel, courtesy of the Library of Congress.*

Henry Clay. *Drawn by A. Gibert from a daguerreotype by P. Haas, courtesy of the Library of Congress.*

had made about abuse of executive powers, calling out Henry Clay and President John Quincy Adams in particular. Besides accusing them both of being dishonest and otherwise immoral, he also derided Clay's ancestors for bringing forth "this being, brilliant yet so corrupt, which, like a rotten mackerel by moonlight, shined and stunk."

But in those days, calling out someone could lead to the literal "calling out" for a duel. And so it was. Clay called him out, and they met for an illegal duel—senators and congressmen were rule-bound to not take what was said in session as "fighting words," lest they fight all the time—on April 8 at four o'clock in the afternoon.

Although Randolph (who had once caned a fellow lawmaker severely for calling him a puppy) had promised another senator that he "had no intention of making Mrs. Clay a widow," he could not promise he would not shoot to kill if he "saw the devil in Clay's eye." It was illegal to duel in Virginia at the time, but Randolph made it part of the terms to duel there so that if he died, he could die on his home soil.

Randolph's gun went off prematurely, firing into the ground. Clay, perhaps thinking Randolph was in earnest, shot at his target when the signal came, blowing a hole in his opponent's deliberately oversized coat. Randolph, wanting to make sure his peaceful intentions could not be misread, fired the next shot into the air. At that point, Clay called off the duel. But before they parted company, he had some words for Randolph:

"I trust in God, my dear sir, you are untouched; after what has occurred, I would not have harmed you for a thousand words." Randolph gestured to his coat and answered coolly, "You owe me a new coat, Mr. Clay." Clay reportedly responded, "I am glad the debt is no greater."

ON THE RUN

Today, the Inn at Gristmill Square (www.gristmillsquare.com) in Warm Springs, Virginia, has a pub named after a man whose life was radically altered by dueling. Simon Kenton was born on Bull Run Mountain in Prince William County. At sixteen, he fought over the honor of a young lady and, believing he had killed his opponent, fled to the west, taking an assumed name. He worked at Warm Springs Mill until 1782, when he discovered his opponent was still alive and he was not wanted for murder, which allowed him to return home.

Simon Kenton (1755–1836). *Courtesy of the New York Public Library Digital Collections.*

During his time away, he served as a scout against the Shawnees in 1774 and saved famous frontiersman Daniel Boone's life in 1777. In 1778, he survived the gauntlet and ritual torture at Chillicothe after being captured. He showed endurance and spirit under torture. Out of respect for his stoicism, he was adopted into the Shawnee tribe, taken as a son by a woman who had lost hers in battle, and given the name Cut-ta-ho-tha (the Condemned Man).

After his second escape, he served in the Northwest Indian War from 1793 to 1794 under General "Mad Anthony" Wayne. In 1799, he led a group of settlers from Kentucky to the Mad River Valley of Ohio, where he had been captured and tortured two decades earlier. Settling in Urbana, Ohio, in 1810, he became brigadier general of the state militia and once again served as an Indian scout in the War of 1812—his life changed utterly because of a duel.

THE JAW BONES CLUB

While rude words and misunderstandings could, under extreme circumstances, lead to offended honor and an untimely demise, most gatherings were more congenial. In Fredericksburg, a group of regular jokesters used to gather at the Farmers' Hotel in the 1830s and 1840s. They called themselves the Jaw Bones Club. Robert Howison wrote that they had all manner of tricks in store for travelers. "Their object," wrote Howison, "was to extract as much enjoyment as possible from any suitable objects for practical jokes."

They sent one gentleman on a roundabout search for the nonexistent "corporation gun" to kill mad dogs. One member specialized in loading unwitting victims' cigars with gunpowder.

WILL YOU TAKE THE PLEDGE?

Not every traveler wanted to participate in such revelry. The Temperance Movement—a push against alcoholic beverages—really hit its stride in the mid-nineteenth century and ran quite the course before culminating in Prohibition. The reasons for its rise were partly practical—fathers and mothers debilitated by alcoholism were one of society's banes. But the rise in abstinence was also partly tied to the rise of religion. John Wesley, the founder of the Methodist Churches, said in the 1700s that "buying, selling, and drinking of liquor, unless absolutely necessary, were evils to be avoided."

Indeed, drunkenness was counted by many a sin, or certainly an invitation to sin and something to be foresworn. Teetotalers would have capital *T*'s written next to their names in temperance pledge books, and it was a movement that swept the country, even if not all partook, particularly those whose cultural gatherings traditionally included alcohol.

As the Third Great Awakening of American Christianity commenced in the late 1850s, indulgence of habitual drunkards decreased, as overindulgence was regarded as frequently leading to sin. Other established temperance societies chose to stress a more fraternal and sympathetic relationship to recovering alcoholics.

This was an extremely popular movement. Even in towns the size of Fredericksburg, several different temperance societies might be meeting—sometimes rival chapters of the same society. In the 1885 Fredericksburg business directory, you will find meetings of the United Lodge, Sons of Sobriety (weekly Wednesday night meetings), and Stonewall Lodge, Sons of Sobriety (weekly Friday night meetings)—an interesting choice of names given the time period, in the aftermath of the Civil War.

SOFT DRINKS FOR THE SOBER

But what does this teetotaling have to do with stagecoaches? While the usual kind of stagecoach tavern would have an ample stock of spirits, self-proclaimed temperance taverns catered to the teetotalers who would certainly prefer to not be in proximity of such temptation. Temperance taverns might sell hospitable yet nonalcoholic cordials, such as elderflower, rosehip and barley water. Those may have faded from general use, but cream soda, root beer and ginger beer/ginger ale are still mainstays. Pharmacist Charles Elmer Hires was an early developer of commercially available nonalcoholic root beer and himself a teetotaler. Indeed, he premiered his root beer at the 1876 U.S. Centennial Exposition as "the temperance drink."

In Virginia, a temperance tavern could be found in Stafford County and is still standing as a private building on Washington Street in Falmouth. An

Temperance tavern, Falmouth Historic District, Stafford County. *Photograph by Jerrye and Roy Klotz, MD.*

advertisement in an 1839 issue of the *Political Arena* mentions the temperance tavern, then called Falls' Temperance House:

> *The Proprietress has, at considerable pains and expense, fitted up, in the best manner, for the accommodation of the Public, the above establishment, in the Town of Falmouth, on strictly temperance principles, where every attention to the comfort of visitors, travelers, and their families, will be dispensed, and no exertion spared to make their stay pleasant and agreeable. Attached to the premises are good Stables and Carriage Houses. Boarders will be received by the week, month, or year, and rooms, fire and lights, furnished, if required. Patronage is respectfully solicited. Refer to B. Gordon and M. Forbes, Esqrs. and Capt. D. Green, Falmouth.*

Temperance taverns could be found elsewhere throughout the state. The November 25, 1837 issue of *Genius of Liberty* ran the following advertisement:

> *Temperance Tavern and Boarding House—The subscriber having opened a House of the above description in Leesburg, at the sign of the Eagle, hopes to be supported by all the members, as well as the friends of the*

Institution. This he especially hopes, as all intemperance will be particularly excluded from the House. He is well provided with a good Ostler [an inn's stableman], *and other servants, and flatters himself that he will be able to give satisfaction to those who may favor him with their patronage, both as to terms and accommodations. Plenty of good Oats and Hay for Horses, and rooms and beds for guests. PRESLY SAUNDERS, Leesburg.*

Following the fashion to be less public about the nature of the public houses, taverns and ordinaries often became known as inns or, to borrow from the French, hotels, lending an air of respectability on the one hand and panache on the other. Today, many of the old taverns have been turned into private homes; some continue to serve local and traveling clientele; some are gone entirely; and a few have been turned into museums showcasing early tavern life. Interestingly, some of newest establishments choose to be called taverns and invoke a touch of historicity, even if Virginia ABC stores only began to open on Sundays quite recently—after the time of traditional church services.

VI
THE GOLDEN AGE OF STAGE TRAVEL

APPLE FRITTERS

PARE some apples, and cut them in thin slices—put them in a bowl, with a glass of brandy, some white wine, a quarter of a pound of pounded sugar, a little cinnamon finely powdered, and the rind of a lemon grated; let them stand some time, turning them over frequently; beat two eggs very light, add one quarter of a pound of flour, a table-spoonful of melted butter and as much cold water as will make a thin batter; drip the apples on a sieve, mix them with the batter, take one slice with a spoonful of batter to each fritter, fry them quickly of a light brown, drain them well, put them in a dish, sprinkling sugar over each, and glaze them nicely.

s the country matured, so did the stagecoach. As a practical means of travel for those without personal fortune, it seemed ideal, its cost subsidized in part by the role it played in delivering the mail.

Oliver Wendell Holmes Sr. (1809–1894)—Harvard-educated poet, physician and general man of letters—had a deep interest in stagecoach transport and realized even then that its history was likely to be lost or only remembered as a symbol of the West. He wrote in his landmark book *Stagecoach East: Stagecoach Days in the East from Colonial Period to the Civil War*:

> *The stagecoach was now an increasingly important part of daily American life. Large numbers of people who previously had never been able to move*

Virginia by Stagecoach

The Trenton coach, 1818. *From Coaches and Coaching Days: A Series of 50, George Arents Collection, New York Public Library Digital Collections.*

far from their homes were traveling the roads from Maine to the Potomac. Commerce, too, benefited enormously, and there was a greater movement of goods and products. And, of course, the mail and the newspapers were carried rapidly by the stages.

Furthermore, there was a certain prestige attached to riding the stages in the early nineteenth century: After all, the proprietors and drivers, with their mail contracts, were acting as agents of the government, and stagecoaches were given the right of way on bridges and ferries. By the 1820s, stagecoaches had begun to take on their best form as the roads became better, and competition between rival stagecoach lines led to an improvement in services generally.

"THE FINEST VEHICLES IN THE WORLD"

About 1820, the stage wagon's design became much more comfortable. Its oval body and rounded top sported a side door—sometimes two—and the body was no longer slamming over hard roads but instead suspended on thoroughbraces, with the driver sitting outside the compartment.

These mail coaches were commonly known as Concord, Albany or Troy coaches, named for their places of manufacture. The earliest new designs may have come out of Albany and Troy, New York, but the most famous would come from a workshop in Concord, New Hampshire. They completely changed the way stagecoach travel was viewed, from a rough necessity to a perfect conveyance for the new nation that reflected its respect for all the people. Here is a description of one of the new style of stagecoaches as was written up proudly in the *Boston American Traveller* in 1825:

Virginia by Stagecoach

Concord-style stage coach at the B&O Museum, Baltimore. *Courtesy of the B&O Museum Collections.*

> *The finest vehicles in the world without any dispute, are stage-coaches. Your sulkys were made for physicians or single gentlemen; your carriage for old maids (or, to be fashionable, "for single ladies advanced",) and old women; your carioles for young children and their nurses; and your gigs, your landaus, and your curricles for fops, dandies and exquisites of both sexes; but your stage-coaches—your downright, modern, well-built stagecoaches—were made for no particular class in society, but for the young, old, the rich and the poor, the great and the small, male and female, of all ranks, and conditions; and whether we ride for health, for pleasure, or for business, we almost invariably prefer one of these carry-alls to any other travelling machine now in vogue.*

These new, comfortable and elegant designs, considered so modern for the time, were the work of innovators. The Concord coaches, built by the Abbot, Downing Company of Concord, New Hampshire, were so well-suited to their purpose that more or less the same design was used into the early twentieth century, and they were the typical coaches used in the Old West.

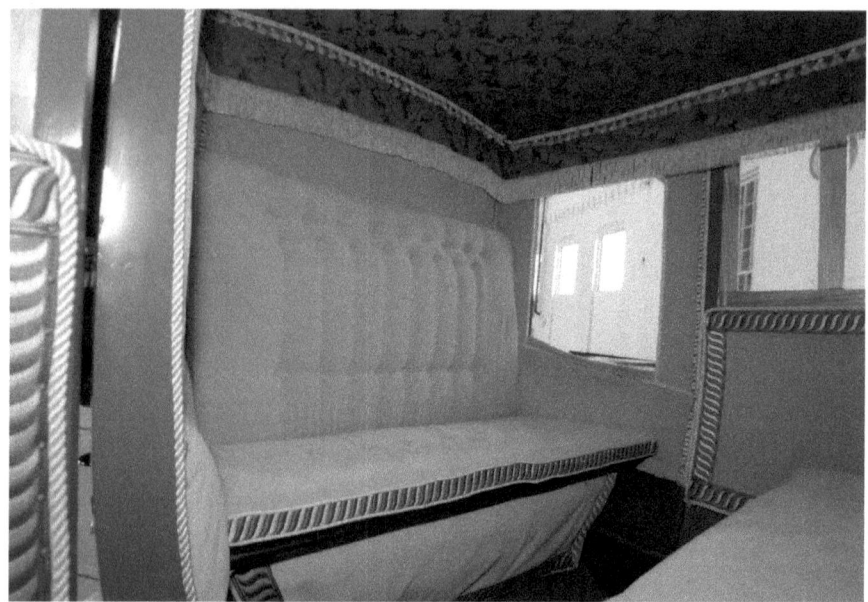

Inside a Concord stage at the B&O Museum, Baltimore. *Courtesy of the B&O Museum Collections.*

CONCORD COACHES TRAVEL THE WORLD

J. Stephens Abbot worked for Lewis Downing when he built the first coach in that style, but he would become a partner. The Abbot, Downing Company of Concord referred to them as mail coaches. Production of this style continued until early in the twentieth century, and the name Concord coach became as well-known and influential as Xerox or Apple, although other manufacturers were turning out similar vehicles.

The Concord coaches were exported around the world, as far as Australia and South Africa, and the Concord designs were naturally copied by other manufacturers. There were quite a few variations in size. Six-, nine- and twelve-passenger sizes were common. From the late 1850s to the mid-1860s, some four-passenger and sixteen-passenger coaches were built—and one that could hold thirty-two passengers. Long seats generally faced one another, and in the larger coaches, there might be one or two more benches between the main seats. There was quite a lot of space for baggage, as there was a rack on top, one on the rear and a space behind the boot.

These new Concord coaches were not drab by any means. Proudly painted in rich, bright colors, they might be decorated with scrollwork and gold

Left: Cobb & Co. thirty-two-passenger heavy Concord coach. *From* Coaches and Coaching Days: A Series of 50, *George Arents Collection, New York Public Library Digital Collections.*

Below: Shelburne Museum's 1852 Concord stagecoach. *Photograph by Lee Wright.*

paint, and their panels often displayed intricate oil paintings of landscapes and other popular subjects. The most usual color was a red body on pale yellow running gear, but other colors might be green, orange, white, blue and more. Hotels might keep their own coaches to convey travelers to train stations, and those were often black or maroon.

BEYOND THE CONCORD

Of course, in addition to the handsome and much-admired Concord stagecoaches, there was a market for less expensive people movers. These kept "wagon" in their names. There were passenger wagons, overland wagons, mud wagons (much hated by Civil War wounded) and mountain wagons. They had space for luggage, too, but not as much, and instead of having a properly constructed compartment to keep out the weather, these, like their predecessors, had open sides. In the event of bad weather, curtains could be rolled down to keep the worst of the rain and mud at bay.

Established stagecoach lines might feature coaches from one manufacturer. For example, the Union Line, which ran in the area of Baltimore and Washington in the 1830s, preferred Albany coaches, which became known as the "Splendid Red Coaches" of the Union Line.

Beltzhoover & Co. owned the Phoenix Line, whose safety coaches ran between Washington and Baltimore in the 1830s, taking about five hours to do so.

Although the Concord coach may be better known today, the Troy coach, built as early as May 1827—a few months before the Concord—was much the same. Manufactured by several firms in Troy, New York, it had excellent improvements over the old type. Charles Veazie's firm added a rooftop luggage rail, while Eaton & Gilbert's added a driver's seat on the roof rather than parallel to the passengers.

A description of that early Troy coach type appeared in the *United States Gazette* in 1831. The "splendid" coach owned by a Mr. Reeside was made in Troy, New York, by Eaton & Gilbert and Charles Veasie:

> *The coach was painted red, and beautifully lined with red morocco. The whole appliances of the carriage were suited to the elegance of the body,*

Phoenix Line's safety coaches traveled from Washington to Baltimore in five hours from 1830 to 1834. *Courtesy of the Library of Congress.*

and bespoke the liberality of the enterprising owner. Mr. Reeside ordered a number of these carriages to be built for the new line that is to commence running between Baltimore and Pittsburgh, by the way of Chambersburg, on the 1st of October.

Troy coaches would be used on the Virginia lines as well. In 1825, the line from Wythe Court House, Virginia, to Greensboro, North Carolina, proclaimed, "The coaches are made at Troy, N.Y., good and comfortable." The rest of the South followed suit.

Why did the Troy coaches become less popularly known as the decades passed than the Concord coaches? According to *America's Early Taverns*, available information suggests the firm of Eaton & Gilbert built more of these stagecoaches than the Abbot, Downing Company, but the former gave up construction much earlier in order to concentrate on manufacturing railway cars.

According to *Stage Coaches and Waggons*, neither a massively strong draft horse was needed for these commercial coaches nor horses with fine looks. Our fond revolutionary Frenchman De Warville noted in 1788 that "the horses used in these carriages (Stage Waggons) are neither handsome nor strong; but they travel very well."

VII
AN AMERICAN WAY OF TRAVEL

SWEET POTATO BUNS

Boil and mash a potato, rub into it as much flour as will make it like bread—add spice and sugar to your taste, with a spoonful of yeast; when it has risen well, work in a piece of butter, bake it in small rolls, to be eaten hot with butter, either for breakfast or tea.

Once stagecoaches began running on regular—and much more frequent!—schedules, it was no longer impractical for the not-so-wealthy without private carriages to plan a visit to see relatives in an adjacent region or state, conduct business, explore cities or simply move themselves to a new neighborhood entirely if reasonably unencumbered.

Colonial America attracted many entrepreneurs, and John Butler was no exception. When his services were no longer needed as a master of the hounds, he took on setting up a stage route. Realizing the need for relatively quick mass transit, in 1756, he outfitted a springless wagon with a rolled cloth top. Boldly painted on the sides were the words "Flying Machine—New York to Philadelphia."

According to *The History of Bucks County, Pennsylvania*, volume 2, Butler's early express service, one of several rival companies, initially ran a stage wagon and stage boat service twice a week. They set out from his house "at the sign of the Death of the Fox, Strawberry alley," on Monday morning, reaching Trenton ferry the same day. Due to the rough ride on plank seats, these early waggons were nicknamed "spankers," although springs would soon be added for some.

Today, the Death of the Fox Inn, which served its public clientele for many years, is a private residence and recognized as a historic landmark, but a brewery has taken up its name and proudly remembers the tavern and stagecoach stop's history.

Thomas Twining, who traveled over the Main Post Road from New York to Washington in 1795, described a ride in one of those aforementioned stage waggons in his 1807 *Notes & Reminiscences*:

> *The vehicle was a long car with four benches. Three of these in the interior held nine passengers, and a tenth passenger was seated by the side of the driver in the front bench. A light roof was supported by eight slender pillars, four on each side. Three large leather curtains suspended on the roof one at each side and the third behind, were rolled up or lowered at the pleasure of the passengers. There was no place nor space for luggage, each person being expected to stow his things as best he could under his seat or legs.*
>
> *The entrance was in front, over the driver's bench. Of course the three passengers in the back seat were obliged to crawl across the other benches to get to their places. There were no backs to the benches to support & relieve us during the rough and fatiguing journey over a newly and ill made road. It would be unreasonable to expect perfection in the arrangements of a new country; but though this rude conveyance was not without its advantages, and was really more suitable to the existing state of American roads than an English stagecoach would have been, it might have been rendered more convenient in some respects without much additional expense. Thus a mere strap behind the seats would have been a great comfort, and the ponderous leather curtains, which extended the whole length of the waggon, would have been much more convenient divided into two or three parts, and with a glass, however small, in each division to give light to the passengers in bad weather, and enable them to have a glimpse of the country. The disposal of the luggage also was extremely incommodious, not only to the owner, but to his neighbors.*

A HORSE FOR A STAGECOACH

For the most part, the breed of the horse did not matter so much as the type. They had to be sturdy animals, capable of pulling a wagon or coach under difficult conditions, and they needed to be strong-hearted so they wouldn't give up. A draft horse, accustomed to heavy work day after day, might seem the perfect choice. But a coach horse needed to be swift as well. For that, a Thoroughbred would surely be the best choice, as they were bred for racing. But Thoroughbreds, as a group, tend to be too high-spirited for the daily grind and teamwork of stagecoaches, besides being prohibitively expensive.

What was needed instead was a horse with speed, strength and a good disposition. In horse-speak, a draft horse is called a cold blood, while a lightweight riding or racing horse is called a hot blood. A mixture of these types would be a warmblood, and a horse of this nature would be well-suited to the role of pulling a stagecoach with endurance and some speed while keeping an even temper. Today, you will find warmbloods in the show ring at the Olympics as well as starring in jumping and dressage trials at horse shows around the world.

Although America does not really have its own warmblood breed per se, European warmbloods include the usually black-coated Friesians, German Oldenburgs, Irish hunters, Swedish warmbloods, Trakehners and more. There is a practical reason for desiring horses without white markings, beyond easily making a good matching team. White markings on the feet are often associated with light-colored hooves, and light hooves are believed to be softer and more easily hurt than darker ones. This holds true for racehorses as well, an old rhyme going:

> *One white foot, buy him.*
> *Two white feet, try him.*
> *Three white feet, be on the sly.*
> *Four white feet, pass him by.*

There is a crueler version of that, but the gist is that a horse with softer feet is likely to break down more under continuous work.

TEAMWORK!

As noted in Colonial Williamsburg's "Stage Waggons and Coaches," the heavier vehicles would typically be pulled by four or six horses, occasionally having a leader in harness at the front to set the pace. Each pair of horses had its own designation. The pair closest to the driver (and the wheels) were

Carriage horses in Colonial Williamsburg. *Author's photograph.*

the "wheel horses" or "wheel team." Horses chosen for this team were preferably steady and strong. They had to be strong enough to pivot the front axle assembly and move the pole from side to side. They also provided the strength for backing and braking. The middle team if there was one was called the "swing team." At the front, there was the "lead team," also known as the "lead horses," capable of setting a brave, quick pace. These lead horses—or horse if a singleton were used—needed to be quick to handle unexpected changes and would be well-trained. In a four-horse hitch, the two teams would simply be the wheel horses and the lead horses.

In horse parlance, horses on the left were considered to be in the "near" position, whereas the ones on the right were "off." This relates to how a rider traditionally mounts a horse, nearly always on the left, and the horses come to expect it. So the left side of the horse—the side of normal approach—is the near side. If a driver said his off wheel horse seemed to have a loose shoe, the farrier would know to check the horse in the back and on the right of the hitch.

Colonial Williamsburg offers visitors a chance to ride in either a reproduction stage waggon or a closed carriage. The carriages are not stagecoaches but rather reproductions of private carriages that would have been used by the gentry.

Josiah Chowning's Tavern in Williamsburg. *Author's photograph.*

THE MAGNIFICENT MORGANS

Traveling well was the bottom line. The horses had to be strong enough to do the work and fast enough to do it quickly and stay on schedule. A four-horse team would be used for larger vehicles, while a smaller vehicle might be drawn by a single team. It was all a matter of what the customer base was as to whether a large or small vehicle was used.

Even so, some coaching lines might prefer to use a particular breed of horse so they made a smart appearance. For instance, John Butterfield, who first ran a line in New York between Albany and Schenectady, chose Morgan horses for his teams. Mostly bay or chestnut in color, they all descend from one horse called Justin Morgan after his owner, a teacher and businessman. Morgans were extremely popular, as they were strong, good-looking, fast and hardy—all ideal qualities for a stagecoach horse.

Justin Morgan was foaled in 1789. His owner called him Figure, but as the stallion's fame grew, he began being known by his master's name. Although his parentage is not officially known, it is believed by many, including the American Morgan Horse Association, that he was sired by True Briton. Descended from mostly Arabian lines, he was an aged horse by the time he sired Figure.

As noted by Mary Lou Wells in *The Illustrated Guide to the Morab Horse*, it seems likely that True Briton was brought over as a hunting horse from

The American Morgan horse—Hale's Green Mountain Morgan. *From Dunton's* Spirit of the Turf, *September 15, 1888.*

England, for he was described by a neighbor to his first master (a British Loyalist) as being set to jump five-foot rail fences to amuse bystanders, and it was the neighbor's understanding that he was, indeed, imported.

True Briton later served his master on the field of battle, as Colonel James Delancey was leader of Westchester County Light Horse ("the Cowboys"). In the midst of war in 1780, the horse was stolen and resold to Selah Norton, who did the patriotic thing and renamed him Beautiful Bay. Norton continued to own him for many years, but he leased him to others to stand at stud, including Justin Morgan in 1785. It is believed that Figure's dam, owned by Morgan, also had Arabian blood, with a possible admixture of Welsh cob accounting for the muscular sturdiness and slight tendency to feathering (lush hair) growing around the fetlocks (ankles).

In any event, Figure proved his strength winning pulling contests against larger draft horses as well as winning relatively short races against champion

Thoroughbreds while still having a sunny disposition. Splendid as he was, perhaps best of all was that these characteristics as well as his good looks were stamped on all of his colts and fillies, creating a hardy new American breed—and one that was perfect for stagecoaches.

RARE BREEDS

Colonial Williamsburg (CW) is visited by thousands of tourists every year, and it has made the decision to showcase rare breeds among its livestock, including its horses. In the past, it has worked with American Cream Draft horses. Although the American Cream did not start as a breed until the early 1900s, the body type is right for the kind of strong draft horse that might have been used in colonial Virginia, and they are very calm and gentle—a must when working with crowds of tourists.

Another rare breed Colonial Williamsburg Foundation previously employed was the Canadian horse. Of medium build and strong, Canadian horses were used for pulling carriages or for riding. They are usually black but may also be bay, brown or chestnut. They are hardy, have good tempers and are thought to be descended from Arabian and Barb lines. Like the Morgan horses, and somewhat similar in build, they were often favorites for pulling stagecoaches in New England.

As of 2018, most of the horses used in CW's tourist area are docile, strong crossbreeds. But Elaine Shirley of Colonial Williamsburg Foundation reports that it is beginning to work with Cleveland Bays. Always a rich brown shade and having only rare white markings, Cleveland Bays were developed during the 1600s in northern England to be very nearly a perfect coach horse. Well-mannered, strong and good-looking, they are particularly known for their hardiness.

Rare as Cleveland Bays are, within the past few decades, several breeding farms have been established in Virginia, including Epiphany Bay Farm in the Hartwood area of Stafford County, Bay Haven Farm/Old Dominion Stud in Loudoun County, Gaylord Cleveland Bays in Berryville and Riverspring Farm in Mount Jackson. In 2006, Old Dominion Stud's Tregoyd Journeyman's ("Joe's") likeness was used for a Breyer horse model.

According to the Cleveland Bay Horse Society of North America, the breed was first imported into Virginia in the early 1800s. The state's Upperville Colt and Horse Show ("the oldest horse show in America") was

Cleveland Bay, 1861. *From* La Connaissance *Générale du Cheval, by Louis Moll and Eugène Gayot.*

begun in 1853 and showcased Colonel Richard Henry Dulany's Cleveland Bay stallion Scrivington and his descendants. Colonel Dulany (1820–1906) owned the Welbourne estate near Middleburg, Virginia. He served in the Seventh Virginia Cavalry's Laurel Brigade during the Civil War. The Upperville Colt and Horse Show is still going strong today—over two thousand horses and riders participate—and takes place in early summer at Grafton Farm, one of Colonel Dulany's original properties.

Unsurprisingly, interest in the breed faltered with the rise of the automobile, but in the 1930s, noted Virginia horseman Alexander Mackay-Smith imported them again to use as foundation stock for hunters. Today, Cleveland Bays are sometimes crossbred with Thoroughbreds to create Cleveland Bay Sport Horses, which are popular for jumping, hunting and dressage.

With the steady inventive improvements from coaches to wagons and finding the most practical methods for conveyance, the stagecoach was a peculiarly American model of what was originally a British institution. In *Stagecoach East*, Oliver Wendell Holmes Sr. remarked:

> *The stagecoach owned the American roads in the East during the first half of the nineteenth century, providing a vast network of transportation for citizens in the young Republic....But the stagecoach was more than a mere mode of transportation; indeed, the eastern stage set the very tempo of American life in that period. It carried the mail and thus became the country's major communications network in those pre-telegraph days. The stagecoach also delivered the newspapers, thereby increasing literacy and disseminating vital information to the public...prior to the Civil War, the Stagecoach played a critical role in forming the social and political climate of the new Republic.*

VIII

A VISIT TO THE SPRINGS

MINT CORDIAL

Pick the mint early in the morning while the dew is on it, and be careful not to bruise it; pour some water over it, and drain it—put two handsful into a pitcher, with a quart of French brandy, cover it, and let it stand till next day; take the mint carefully out, and put in as much more, which must be taken out next day—do this the third time: then put three quart of water to the brandy, and one pound of loaf sugar powdered; mix it well together—and when perfectly clear, bottle it.

The Virginia Tidewater gentry patterned themselves after the English gentry in many respects, Revolution or not, what with their love of horseracing, balls, gambling and so on. One of their great pleasures, particularly in the eighteenth and nineteenth centuries, was a visit to "take the waters" at a spa, usually situated in a resort town with a natural spring renowned for its healing properties.

Tidewater Virginia, being situated on an alluvial coastal plain, doesn't lend itself to natural springs. That and its climate, particularly near the swampier regions (they do call it the Dismal Swamp), make for an unpleasant and potentially unhealthy experience, especially during the warmer months. How fortunate that just a few days' journey from them was the Shenandoah Valley with its cooler temperatures and limestone underpinnings. Permeable as limestone is, it naturally forms both fascinating caverns and mineral springs, believed to be wellsprings of health by a sometimes-desperate populace in the days before antibiotics and other modern treatments.

Enterprising owners built cabins, cottages and hotels to house and feed the hopeful travelers. Eventually, "the season" at the springs (which ran from July through early September) was the hope of many an invalid—and matchmaking mama.

WHITE SULPHUR SPRINGS

The Greenbrier

From the late eighteenth to the almost mid-nineteenth century, stagecoaches were the way the middle class (without private carriages) would travel to take the cure. The accommodations varied wildly depending on what was available—and often very little was available. In the opening chapter to Perceval Reniers's *The Springs of Virginia*, an unfortunate stagecoach passenger must plead his case when there is very likely no room at the inn:

> *When George W. Featherstonhaugh, F.R.S., F.G.S., arrived at the White Sulphur Springs (now The Greenbrier) in August, 1834, he was possessed by an idea. The idea was, when the coach stopped, to leap out ahead of all the other passengers, and the object of that was to beat them to the "man in brown." Forewarned was forearmed. Over at the Warm Springs the Kentucky lady had told him how it would be. The White Sulphur was crowded to repletion, she said, and no matter how respectable you were, if you didn't come in your own carriage you were turned away without ceremony. The only possible way to get in at all was to wring the promise of a cabin from the man in brown. He controlled everything. And, said the lady from Kentucky, "if he wasn't the biggest liar that ever belonged to Virginia there was a great one to be born yet."*

Sadly for Featherstonhaugh, he did arrive by stagecoach, not surprising given that he had come from England to travel in the United States. It was the height of the season for the springs, and Major Anderson ("the man in brown"), a short, heavy-set gentleman who was indeed dressed in brown and wore a tall, greasy beaver hat set at an extreme angle, was being pressed from all sides, as it was the time of day when the masses arrived by several stagecoaches at White Sulphur.

Hotel, White Sulphur Springs, West Virginia, 1900–15. *By the Detroit Publishing Company, courtesy of the Library of Congress.*

Major Anderson—also known a bit ironically as the little Grand Vizier as well as the Metternich of the Mountains (Metternich being a prince and imperial Austria's chancellor)—was having none of the pleas and entreaties, including Featherstonhaugh's. There was simply no room, "Not room for a cat, to say nothing of your family." Featherstonhaugh might have preferred to have been driven on to a less crowded resort, but by that time, the stagecoach driver had already unloaded his luggage and his family. So they were sent to "quarantine"—lodging at local neighborhood houses until they could work their way into the Metternich's good graces.

The Featherstonhaugh family initially found a perch at the home of a blacksmith turned tavern keeper. It was another five days before the family would be shuffled into a one-room cottage on a non-fashionable section of the resort called Alabama Row before moving on to Compulsion Row. The latter was in the process of being built to accommodate those unlucky worthies who were shunted down from the more desirable Paradise Row and

Caroline Row, where the cottage owners, who could return unexpectedly, had the power to evict temporary residents.

The Metternich had tried to shoo his overflow of guests along to less wildly popular resorts, such as Blue Sulphur Springs, but to no avail. White Sulphur Springs was widely considered the place to see and be seen. Never mind the waters' purported health benefits. Like Bath in England, all of the fashionable people—and those who aspired to be fashionable—were here.

The hotel, built on the Greenbrier's property in 1857, was called the "Old White." It had a dining room that could accommodate 1,200 guests and was considered the largest in the country. Before the Civil War, five presidents had stayed at the "Presidents' Cottage:" Martin Van Buren, John Tyler, Millard Fillmore, Franklin Pierce and James Buchanan. After the Civil War, they kept coming—twenty-seven in total so far. Today, the Greenbrier at White Sulphur Springs maintains the Presidents' Cottage Museum and also offers tours to guests and the general public of its now-declassified Cold War bunker. The Greenbrier was to be the last resort of a besieged Congress and included a fallout shelter. For decades, its existence was considered a well-founded rumor, but now it can be seen.

Of course, the Greenbrier's major draw is still the beauty, rest, recreation and hospitality in its historic mountain setting.

BLUE SULPHUR SPRINGS

Blue Sulphur Springs (also in Greenbrier County) was no doubt delightful in its own way, even if it was perhaps not quite as desirable as White Sulphur Springs. Today, its Greek pavilion is all that remains of the extensive structures, which once included two brick buildings attached to a continuous range of two- and three-story structures. Its fountain of healing waters was enclosed in marble slabs.

One of the ways Blue Sulphur was not delightful was the architecture. Dr. William Burke—who owned Red Sulphur Springs and wrote *The Mineral Springs of Western Virginia* (reprinted in 1846) as a guide to would-be patients—thought the service and furnishings were fine, but as to its buildings' design and layout:

> *Never have we seen bad taste more unfortunately illustrated than here. It seems as if the designer had his brain obfuscated by mint-julap. What*

man in his sober senses could have ever thought of spoiling a lovely valley like this, admitting a prospect of several miles, by throwing across it from hill to hill a long line of buildings which could have been so easily and so gracefully ranged along the sides; not only obstructing the view, but also preventing the delightful current of air which otherwise would have fanned it in the dog-days?*

Those buildings at Blue Sulphur would not be standing much longer. During the Civil War, all of them were destroyed except for the pavilion, a three-story Greek Revival structure.

SWEET SULPHUR SPRINGS

"Old Sweet"

There were many resorts at mineral springs, including the much-loved "Old Sweet." Located in Monroe County, West Virginia, Sweet Sulphur Springs was supposedly discovered by Europeans in 1764, the first of the springs to come to their attention. In Dr. William Burke's opinion, these mineral waters were too strong for people suffering from lung-related illnesses or women either "in a delicate condition" (pregnant) or prone to severe periodic bleeding. But he believed the waters were wonderful for otherwise healthy aged persons, who would "find youth and vigor and elasticity at the bottom of this noble fountain."

In its earlier incarnation, visitors would stay at log cabins, but by 1842, Dr. John B. Lewis—who owned Sweet Springs and was its resident physician—had built a handsome house as well as brick and framed cottages for visitors.

Old Sweet was a favorite place for friends to gather and precarious health to be restored. In a 1791 letter, Secretary of State Thomas Jefferson wrote: "I shall be happy to hear that Mrs. Skipwith's stay at Richmond has bettered her health, & that the trip to the Sweet springs shall do it still more."

Sweet Springs' first owner was James Moss in 1760, and its first proprietor was William Lewis. Among the notables to try Sweet Springs were George and Martha Washington, Thomas Jefferson, Patrick Henry, Henry Clay, James and Dolley Madison, Robert E. Lee and many more.

At first, there were only log cabins for the guests, but by 1792, there was a hotel, and later there would be two-story brick cottages. There is a legend that the first mint julep was concocted there.

Former guesthouses at Sweet Springs. *Photograph by Carol G. Highsmith, courtesy of the Library of Congress.*

Bathhouse colonnade at Sweet Springs. *Photograph by Carol G. Highsmith, courtesy of the Library of Congress.*

Naturally, visitors were down in the years immediately following the Civil War, but by the 1880s, a lot of the trade had come back. An 1887 advertisement noted that it offered billiards, polo, telegraph service, religious service, croquet and ten-pin bowling.

Old Sweet at last closed in 1928. It was not as accessible as the Greenbrier, which had better railroad connections as of 1869 (to Richmond) and 1873 (to Ohio). The Greenbrier did not require a carriage or stagecoach ride for travelers to get there. For a time, Sweet Springs maintained its medicinal connections and was used as a tuberculosis sanitarium. It was purchased by the state in 1945 and run as an old-age home—the Andrew S. Rowan Memorial Home—until 1991.

In 2005, it was sold to a private owner, who had hopes of reopening it as a resort, spa and conference center, but apparently that was not a success, as it was sold again at auction in 2015. Its new owner, Ashby Berkley, had spent decades restoring and operating Pence Springs Hotel in Summers County. Ready for another project, he has taken on Sweet Springs. Berkley formed a 501(c) nonprofit, Sweet Springs Resort Park, which will allow it to qualify for such things as state historic preservation grants, and it is hoped Old Sweet will see better days.

Ashby Berkley's previous project at Pence Springs has its own interesting history. In its day, Pence Springs was known far and wide for its water. Andrew Pence began bottling it in 1882, and it won a silver medal at the 1904 World's Fair in St. Louis. Pence Springs was fortunate to be only about a mile away from the Chesapeake & Ohio (C&O) Railroad, making shipping the spring water a practical proposition. In Pence Springs, the 1918 hotel that Berkley took on had seen duty for several decades as a state women's prison. Once it had undergone a major renovation, it became home to the Greenbrier Academy for Girls.

So how would time be spent at a fashionable spring resort when not actually taking the waters? As Perceval Reniers archly observed at White Sulphur Springs, there was a standard daily progression in this "forest opera:"

> *The flood and ebb tides of this movement were fairly regular, since the worshippers of Hygeia enjoyed doing the same thing at the same hours. They moved through the day's glad ritual together and one day was much like another: the same three mass attacks on the springhouse and on the dining room, the same plantation lull every afternoon ("evening" in their language), the same leisurely promenade after siesta, the same drift to the ballroom after a supper which was usually called "tea."*

Like their English counterparts, the more fashionable springs were places where the young gentry might meet their future mates. As to those not interested in matrimony, conversation and card games abounded.

Other resorts in the southwestern part of Virginia included Dagger's Springs (Dibrell's Spring) in Botetourt County; Hot Springs, now home to the luxurious Homestead resort; Red Sulphur Springs (owned by Dr. William Burke) in Monroe County; Red Sweet Springs near Sweet Springs in Alleghany County; Rockbridge Alum Springs in Rockbridge County; Salt Sulphur Springs in Monroe County (written up in a pamphlet by famed surgeon Dr. Thomas Mütter); Warm Springs in Bath County, later called Jefferson Pools; and Berkeley Springs.

WARM SPRINGS

While Thomas Jefferson did take the waters at Warm Springs, he did not experience salubrious effects. Writing to Colonel William Alston, a companion during his time there in August 1818:

> *I became seriously affected afterwards by the continuance of the use of the waters. They produced imposthume* [abscess], *eruption, with fever, colliquative sweats and extreme debility. These sufferings, aggravated by the torment of long & rough roads, reduced me to the lowest stage of exhaustion by the time I got home. I have been on the recovery some time, & still am so; but not yet able to sit erect for writing.*

Warm Springs, Bath County, Virginia, 1840. *Courtesy of the New York Public Library Digital Collections.*

SALT SULPHUR SPRINGS

"Old Salt"

"Old Salt" in Monroe County, West Virginia, was another favorite. Its "Old Stone Hotel" there, dating to 1821, has been gently renovated in the past few decades to serve as a private residence. Old Salt was the favored resort of South Carolinians. It featured Southern-style food as well as a grand ballroom with a musicians' gallery. An 1835 gazetteer remarked on the excellence of the accommodations and the polite and obliging dispositions of its owners.

After the Late Unpleasantness, Old Salt was run by a former Union officer from 1882 until his death in 1913. Colonel J.W.M. Appleton was noted for his "Yankee initiative." He took it upon himself to establish a stagecoach line connecting the resort to the closest C&O railroad station. After Colonel Appleton's demise, Old Salt never quite regained its resort status.

Salt Sulphur Springs, Virginia. *Courtesy of the Library of Congress.*

CHAPMAN SPRINGS

The first permanent settlement in Giles County was initially known as Gunpowder Springs for the permeating smell of sulphur. In the 1830s, the Hygaean Springs resort began nearby. Its name was changed to Chapman Springs when Dr. David Johnston Chapman took charge of it in 1853. According to *Lost Communities of Virginia*, daily stagecoaches connected Chapman's Springs (later called New River White Sulphur Springs) with Yellow Sulphur Springs and Montgomery White Sulphur Springs.

Captain William Eggleston took over Chapman's Springs in 1867, giving it and the nearby town his name. In 1870, the Virginia General Assembly incorporated the New River White Sulphur Springs Turnpike Company, which raised funds to construct a road connecting the railroad at New River to the nearby springs. Still, rather than take the stagecoach ride, some visitors opted for a smoother route, debarking from the train at New River depot and taking flat-bottomed boats to the springs. Eggleston's resort survived until the 1930s.

FAUQUIER WHITE SULPHUR SPRINGS

Much farther north, in what we now call Northern Virginia, there stood Fauquier White Sulphur Springs, also known as Warrenton Springs or Lee Springs. In its heyday, it could handle up to eight hundred people and was resorted to as a meeting place by the Virginia state legislature during the Richmond cholera outbreak of 1849. As written up in the *Richmond Whig* newspaper, the taxpayers had some concerns:

> *After a week's wrangling the wise and heroic gentlemen who were, last winter, intent upon fighting the Abolitionists, have fled, from the bare apprehension of Cholera. They meet next Monday at Fauquier Springs; What the good people of Virginia, who will have to pay the expenses of this jaunt to a fashionable watering-place, will think of it is yet to be ascertained.*

In a broadside dating to the mid-1840s, Fauquier Springs advertised that visitors could enjoy "A first-rate band of Music—spacious Ball Rooms and Parlors—extensive porticos, and paved walks—a well supplied table and bar,

Hotel at Fauquier Sulphur Springs, Virginia. *Photograph by Timothy H. O'Sullivan at the second battle of Bull Run, July–August 1862, courtesy of the Library of Congress.*

and almost every species of legitimate amusement, unite in driving 'dull care away,' while the climate and the waters improve the health."

Hundreds of people descended on each of these springs during the season, and quite a number arrived by stagecoach. They might visit one and stay for some time—Jefferson's unfortunate visit to Warm Springs lasted several weeks—or make a round of them, trying the medicinal properties of each one, making Dr. William Burke's publication ever so useful. Later on, railroads would be used to shorten the trip to some of the springs, although a stagecoach might be needed to complete the journey.

With the rise of more effective pharmaceutical and surgical treatments throughout the twentieth century, the desperate need to find any possible cure for long-lived maladies decreased and so did the perceived medicinal need for the springs. Today, many of the springs are simply abandoned with most of their buildings gone. But you can still get a literal taste of the mineral waters—or, if you prefer, submerge yourself—at the Greenbrier (White Sulphur Springs), the Homestead (Hot Springs) or Berkeley Springs in what is now northern West Virginia.

IX
DARK REFLECTIONS

TO FRY PERCH

Clean the fish nicely, but do not take out the roes, dry them on a cloth, sprinkle some salt, and dredge them with flour, lay them separately on a board; when one side is dry, turn them, sprinkle salt and dredge the other side; be sure the lard boils when you put the fish in, and fry them with great care; they should be a yellowish brown when done. Send melted butter or anchovy sauce in a boat.

A PAINFUL HISTORY

The springs' genteel lifestyle, as well as much of the prosperity of the South, came with a significant human cost. Chapman Springs, which was renamed New River White Sulphur Springs in 1858, underwent a series of improvements during the run-up to the Civil War, including a new hotel and dance pavilion. Guests could expect comfort and good times, and if they did not bring their own servants (slaves) with them, the resorts would have unpaid as well as paid staff to see to their needs.

Any time a grand occasion is described, whether they are specifically included in the description or not, there would be servants filling glasses, cooking food, serving it and cleaning the quarters. A drawing done at Chapman Springs in July 1853 illustrates this. Entitled *The Party at Supper & Breakfast, Chapman Springs*, it is a simple watercolor depicting an enslaved woman and boy serving food to a large table of resort guests, while another

Dicey's Cottage, believed to be slave quarters, adjacent to the Lafayette Inn & Restaurant, Stanardsville. *Author's photograph.*

slave tends to fans to keep the party cool. The drawing is somewhat crude, but it effectively conveys and preserves a moment in time. As constituted, the springs absolutely relied on slave labor to function.

Though the quality of a slave's life would vary from situation to situation, the endemic evils of that "peculiar institution" were ever-present, as they served in grand houses, in town houses, on the docks, in the workshops, in the fields and in so many ways behind the reins and behind the scenes at every stagecoach stop and on every turnpike. Slave labor was also used to build and maintain the roads. As for the stagecoach drivers, they might be white or black, free or slave.

THE MADDENS MADE THEIR OWN WAY

Although it was illegal for free African Americans to own taverns before the Civil War, exceptions were made—or rather, a clever system was devised whereby those partaking would be considered guests paying for the right to sleep over on the land. The fee just happened to include the cost of spirits consumed. In *We Were Always Free: The Maddens of Culpeper County, Virginia: A 200-Year History*, descendant T.O. Madden Jr. set down how the Madden family began with an Irish girl named Mary Madden who bore a child, Sarah, said to be fathered by a slave belonging to Colonel James Madison (the father of President James Madison).

Sarah worked for Madison until she paid off the fine incurred by her birth, as the law decreed. In 1750, indentured women servants who had illegitimate children by "a Negro or mulatto" were liable for a fifteen-pound fine for the use of the parish or sale of the servants for five years after the expiration of their original indenture. The children of such unions were to be bound out as servants until they reached the age of thirty-one. And that is what happened to Mary's daughter Sarah Madden.

When finally free, she and the youngest of her ten children, Willis, stayed together. She worked as a seamstress and a laundress, eventually earning enough to become, with her son, a dairy farmer and tavern keeper. Their Madden's Tavern was also popular with drovers. *We Were Always Free* is unusual in its detail because it is based not on conjecture but on papers carefully saved down through the generations, including the travel passes, papers of indenture, freedom papers and records from Sarah's laundry business, all saved in an old hide-bound trunk.

Virginia by Stagecoach

"THE CURSES OF THIS HORRIBLE INSTITUTION"

When famous English author Charles Dickens came to tour America in 1842, his sometimes mode of transport was the stagecoach. Like many travelers of this period, he took a steamboat from Washington to Belle Plain on Potomac Creek in Stafford County. From there, it was the stagecoach connection to Fredericksburg, where he could get on a train to the state's capital in Richmond. It was a memorable ride into Fredericksburg but not in a good way:

> *Soon after nine o'clock we come to Potomac Creek, where we are to land; and then comes the oddest part of the journey. Seven stage-coaches are preparing to carry us on. Some of them are ready, some of them are not ready. Some of the drivers are blacks, some whites. There are four horses to each coach, and all the horses, harnessed or unharnessed are there.*
>
> *The passengers are getting out of the steamboat, and into the coaches; the luggage is being transferred in noisy wheelbarrows; the horses are frightened, and impatient to start....The coaches are something like the French coaches, but not nearly so good. In lieu of springs, they are hung on bands of the strongest leather.*
>
> *There is very little choice or difference between them; and they may be likened to the car portion of the swings at an English fair, roofed, put upon axle-trees and wheels, and curtained with painted canvas. They are covered with mud from the roof to the wheel-tire, and have never been cleaned since they were first built....The first half-mile of the road is over bridges made of loose planks laid across two parallel poles, which tilt up as the wheels roll over them; and In the river. The river has a clayey bottom and is full of holes, so that half a horse is constantly disappearing unexpectedly, and can't be found again for some time.*
>
> *But we get past even this, and come to the road itself, which is a series of alternate swamps and gravel-pits....And so we do the ten miles or thereabouts in two hours and a half; breaking no bones, though bruising a great many...*
>
> *This singular kind of coaching terminates at Fredericksburgh, whence there is a railway to Richmond.*

Charles Dickens spent time at the Farmers' Hotel. His visit brought a lot of excitement. As ten-year-old Moncure Daniel Conway recorded, he was

White seaman and colored man on board steamboat on the Potomac from Washington to Aquia Creek, Virginia, June 26, 1853. *By George Wallis, courtesy of the Library of Congress.*

"Boz" (Charles Dickens), 1839.
Lithograph by Eliphalet M. Brown, courtesy of the Library of Congress.

determined to see the famous author, so much so that he jumped out an open window—seven or eight feet from the ground—at Thomas Hanson's Fredericksburg Classical and Mathematical Academy, located in the north wing of old city hall.

Young Conway, who would grow up to become a well-known author himself (although he is remembered today more as a determined abolitionist), thought the flogging he received on his return to school worth the privilege of getting a good look at "the greatest man in the world."

His hero, Charles Dickens, also took a very dim view of the institution of slavery. He observed more of its demeaning effects from his railway car:

The tract of country through which it takes its course was once productive; but the soil has been exhausted by the system of employing a great amount of slave labour in forcing crops, without strengthening the land: and it is now little better than a sandy desert overgrown with trees. Dreary and uninteresting as its aspect is, I was glad to the heart to find anything on which one of the curses of this horrible institution has fallen; and had greater pleasure in contemplating the withered ground, than the richest and most thriving cultivation in the same place could possibly have afforded me.

In this district, as in all others where slavery sits brooding, (I have frequently heard this admitted, even by those who are its warmest advocates) there is an air of ruin and decay abroad, which is inseparable from the system. The barns and outhouses are mouldering away; the sheds are patched and half roofless; the log cabins (built in Virginia with external chimneys made of clay or wood) are squalid in the last degree. There is no look of decent comfort anywhere. The miserable stations by the railway side; the great wild wood-yards, whence the engine is supplied with fuel; the negro children rolling on the ground before the cabin doors, with dogs and pigs; the biped beasts of burden slinking past: gloom and dejection are upon them all.

In the negro car belonging to the train in which we made this journey, were a mother and her children who had just been purchased; the husband

and father being left behind with their old owner. The children cried the whole way, and the mother was misery's picture. The champion of Life, Liberty, and the Pursuit of Happiness, who had bought them, rode in the same train; and, every time we stopped, got down to see that they were safe.

But times were changing, albeit slowly. In just a few months, the railway would join the steamboat landing at Aquia in Stafford to a new rail line that would run to Fredericksburg, eliminating the need to take the stage from the Belle Plain landing to town.

Much more significantly, slavery would be gone within twenty-five years, after the great bloodshed of the Civil War, much of it centered in this region. Indeed, young Moncure Conway, who had followed his mother's antislavery sentiments and had been educated in the North, succeeded in freeing thirty of his father's slaves in 1862, in the midst of the Civil War. They traveled to Ohio where they became known as "the Conway Colony" at the village of Yellow Springs in Greene County.

A PIECE OF THE PAST

Coaching inns and taverns were gathering places for public events. As taverns were centers for the community and, in some communities, the only public buildings, they were places for anything that might draw a crowd—and that might include public hangings and slave sales.

It is difficult to step away from the past, and many believe it is important to remember it, no matter how painful. Fredericksburg's slave auction block, in front of where the old Planters Hotel once stood, faces an uncertain future. Though vandalized in 2005, it stands on the corner of Charles and William Streets—for now—as a reminder of a darker chapter in the state's history. At the time of the vandalism, Cedric Rucker of Historic Fredericksburg Foundation Inc. told the local newspaper: "We should be telling all of our stories, not just the pretty part."

Today, community discussions are trying to get a consensus on the best way to tell that story. There are plans to move the block to the Fredericksburg Area Museum, on the corner of William and Princess Anne Streets.

X
"IF GOD PERMITS..."

WHEN THINGS WENT WRONG

CORN MEAL BREAD

Rub a piece of butter the size of an egg, into a pint of corn meal—make it a batter with two eggs, and some new milk—add a spoonful of yeast, set it by the fire an hour to rise, butter little pans, and bake it.

In *Rivers and Roads*, the author quotes 1790s Virginia visitor Isaac Weld: "if persons wish to travel with comfort, they ought always to set out provided with cushions for their hips and elbows, otherwise they cannot expect but to receive numberless contusions."

"IT IS THE FIRST NIGHT THAT COSTS"

Presumably, things were better by 1869, for in that year, the September issue of *New York Coach-maker's Magazine* recalled the bad old days:

> The term, stages, is associated with a long catalogue of calamities, inconveniences and horrors, almost insupportable. A stage is a heavy, unwieldy vehicle, generally drawn by four jaded horses, urged along by a vulgar, insolent driver. There are some exceptions, some drivers being respectable, and some stages are mere lumber wagons.
>
> In stage-riding it is peculiarly true that it is the first night that costs. It is more intolerable than the succeeding half-dozen, were the journey

prolonged for a week; the breaking-in is fearful, the prolongation is bearable. The air gets cold; the road grows dusty and chokes, or rough and alarms you; the legs gets stiff and numb; the temper edges; everybody is overcome with sleep, but can't stay asleep—the struggle of contending nature racks every nerve, fires every feeling; everybody flounders and knocks about against everybody else in helpless despair; perhaps the biggest man in the stage will really get asleep, which doing, he involuntarily and with irresistible momentum spreads himself legs, boots, arms and head, over the whole inside of the coach; the girls screech; the profane swear, some lady wants a smelling-bottle out of her bag, and her bag is somewhere on the floor—nobody knows where—but found it must be; everybody's back hair comes down, and what is nature and what is art in costume and character revealed—and then, hardest trial of all, morning breaks upon the scene and the feelings—everybody dirty, grim, faint, "all to pieces," cross—such a disenchanting exhibition!

Stage waggons used thoroughbraces—heavy, layered straps that passed under the bottom of the vehicle—to offset the rough ride a coach might naturally give, allowing the carriage compartment to swing independent of the pounding the undercarriage was taking on rough roads. Unfortunately, this action put a lot of strain on the thoroughbraces, especially as the coaches were often heavily loaded with passengers and baggage.

THOSE INVENTIVE AMERICANS

Stage Coaches and Waggons quotes English traveler John Melish, who wrote in 1812: "The defect was supplied by breaking down an honest man's fence, and thrusting a rail under the body of the carriage, while the passengers stood almost up to the ankles in the mud, holding it up."

Another Englishman, John Duncan, wrote in more detail in 1819:

The road through which we drove (it was literally through) had shaken our wagon, that after nine hours of jolting one of the straps gave way, and we were brought to a stand by the carriage sinking down upon the pole. Americans are not easily disconcerted. There was a rail fence by the road side, from which the driver selected a stout rafter long enough to reach from the footboard in front to the after axle, the body of the wagon was hove up by our united efforts, and the wooden substitute was thrust under it. We then resumed our seats and jolted on, quite unconscious of any additional inconvenience from riding on a rail.

But what if there were no fence rails to be filched? Tyrone Power (not the Hollywood actor) told of a solution in 1836:

We broke [a thoroughbrace] *by a sudden plump, into a hole, that would have shaken a broad-wheeled wagon into shavings. Our driver did not approve of any of the fence-rails in the vicinity, so plunged into the wood, accompanied by one of my western companions; and in ten minutes they returned, bearing a young hickory pole, that the driver assured us was "as tough as Andrew Jackson himself and as hard to break, though it might give a little under a heavy load." This was shoved under the body of the carriage, and rested on the fore and hind axles; it was lashed fast, and the spare part of the spar was left sticking out behind, like the end of the main boom of a smack. The coach body when rested upon this, was found to have a considerable list to port...* [but] *the driver was enabled by this ingenious substitute for a carriage spring to "go ahead."*

Fence rails might also be used as a kind of jack if the part of the axle known as the king bolt snapped. That would have to be replaced by a proper substitute, but a brace of fence rails could lift the whole body so the new king bolt could be put into place.

Naturally, missing sections of fencing could lead livestock to break through what fencing remained and wander into the road, but that was a problem for another driver.

Another frequent accident could be caused by the iron around the wheels being loosened by jolting, causing the whole wheel to collapse. Depending on the speed and the terrain, passengers might be severely injured.

But the journey must, if at all possible, go on. Royal Navy officer Captain Frederick Marryat—also a novelist, inventor and

Frederick Marryat, British naval officer and novelist. *Photograph by Sophus Williams, Ernst Hader, artist, courtesy of the Library of Congress.*

scientist—was rather taken with his fellow travelers' inventiveness: "The Americans are never at a loss when they are in 'The fix.' The passengers borrowed an axe; and in a short time wedges were cut from one of the trees at the road-side, and the wheel was so well repaired that it lasted us the remainder of the journey."

Although it wasn't on every journey, the rough American roads meant "upsets" were fairly unavoidable for travelers on anything but the main roads.

Marryat also wrote: "The drivers are very skillful...and if you are upset, it is generally more the fault of the road than the driver. No one thinks anything of an upset in America....These mischances must be expected in a new country."

FROM A MOUNTAIN ROAD TO THE PATHS OF THE SEA

Another naval officer—this one an American, and a famous one at that—experienced a serious stagecoach accident whose end result was a great gain for all the world's navies. Matthew Fontaine Maury, born in Spotsylvania, Virginia, in 1806, was assigned to the USS *Vincennes*, a U.S. warship that was the first of its kind to circumnavigate the globe. This journey sparked an interest in navigation.

Very fit for duty at sea and keen on exploring, he likely would have been a fine ship's captain in time were it not for a stagecoach accident. While traveling by stage on perilous mountain roads, he gave up his seat inside the coach to an elderly black woman. Perched—along with others—on top of the coach, he took a very bad fall during its upset, severely breaking a leg. He recovered after some time, but his fitness for active duty was never the same. Being reassigned to work stateside, he made a thorough study of navigation, being inspired to chart "the paths of the sea," partially by Psalms 8:8: "The fowl of the air, and the fish of the sea, and whatsoever passeth through the paths of the sea." In time, Maury would earn the nickname "Pathfinder of the Seas."

"INDESCRIBABLE"

While it's true that the hard-used coaches (and horses) could break down, the roads themselves could cause an upset even if everything else was in perfect working condition. There were hills to climb, streams to cross and pedestrians and other vehicles—many slow and lumbering—to be avoided. In rainy weather, trees would fall across lanes lit only by the light of the moon—if visible—and whatever light the coaches could carry themselves. Another problem in the rainy season was swollen streams, and bad drainage on a road could turn it into a stream at points.

John Randolph of Roanoke, our duelist/statesman from a previous chapter, gave his terse, ultimate verdict on one frequently traveled road—and he was presumably in a private carriage:

> *Dec. 12th, Wednesday. Hard frost. Left Fredericksburg at nine, A.M. Reached Stafford, C.H., at half-past eleven, Dumfries at five minutes past three, P.M., and Occoquon at half-past five. I made no stop except to breathe the horses, from Dumfries to Neabsco, sixty-five minutes three and a half miles. The five miles beyond Dumfries employed nearly two hours. Roads indescribable.*
> *—John Randolph of Roanoke, 1821*

The weary traveler may have passed by a certain well-established tavern. Also known as Love's Tavern, the Brick Tavern, the Stage Coach Inn and Old Hotel, Williams Ordinary is still standing just off Route 1 in Dumfries. New dendrochronological evidence suggests that it dates to the 1780s. It served clientele who used the "rolling road" to get their goods to market, including rolling hogsheads (round barrels five feet tall), hence the name. Now housing Prince William County's Historic Preservation Division, it was first used as a store by John Glassford and Company. George Washington stopped by the storehouse to resupply on his way to the Revolution's last battle at Yorktown. It became a tavern or ordinary a few years after the war. It is a very handsome structure with stone quoins around the doorway. It is thought to be Virginia's only surviving colonial building with all-head-bond brickwork.

Williams Ordinary, Main Street, Dumfries, Prince William County, Virginia, ca. 1933. *Courtesy of the Historic American Buildings Survey, Library of Congress.*

A RACE TO THE TOP

What with nature's hazards of ice, snow, rain, mud and windstorms, surely the drivers wouldn't go looking for more trouble—but some of them did.

Rival stagecoach lines might run on the same road at very nearly the same time. Often there were not enough passengers to keep two (or more) lines in business, so competition was key to survival. Competing lines would advertise their faster times. Plus, in later decades, they all had to make their connections with arriving steamboats and trains.

If, on a narrow road, a stagecoach met its rival and wished to pass, a race might very well ensue, and the results could be disastrous, with the losers sometimes being overturned into a ditch.

Although some passengers may have gotten into the spirit of it, understandably, the majority did not. Newspapers ran editorials against it, and some stagecoach lines began advertising that they had changed their hours of departure so as to not align exactly with their competition. In some states, laws were passed, but out on the open road, very nearly anything might happen.

"Springing Them Up to Meet the Train." *By James Pollard (1792–1867), courtesy of the Library of Congress.*

HIGHWAY ROBBERY

That "anything" might include highway robbery. According to "Stage Waggons and Coaches," if a coach did not have accompanying outriders or passengers riding topside, it might be a rather simple thing for someone to ride up behind an overloaded stagecoach and cut free a few of the smaller pieces of luggage en route. Unless these small robberies were routine along the same routes, the perpetrators would probably get away with it. After all, it wasn't the U.S. mail, which frequently included large sums of money moving from town to town. "Great Mail" pouches carried between large commercial centers might contain $50,000 or $100,000. As there were no travelers' checks for safety or easy ways to replenish funds at a destination, better-heeled passengers could be a fruitful source of illicit income as well. But the price of highway robbery of the Great Mail was high indeed. The Post Office Act of 1792 made it a death sentence, and the Act of 1799 only mollified it a bit, changing the penalty for the first offence to forty lashes (only possibly lethal) plus

The Piedmont Mail Route (seen on May 1, 1832) ran from Washington City to Milledgeville, Georgia, paralleling the Blue Ridge. *Courtesy of the Library of Congress.*

imprisonment not to exceed ten years. However, the penalty for a second go at the mail was still death, as it was in a first instance when the driver's life was threatened with dangerous weapons.

As described in *Stagecoach Days and Stagecoach Kings*, robberies of passengers on the National Road from Pennsylvania to Ohio were not terribly unusual and often followed a set routine. At the top of a steep hill, when the horses were pulling slowly, two armed, masked men would emerge. One would grab the near lead horse's reins. One would brandish pistols at the stagecoach and order the driver to stop. If he did not do so, he would likely be shot. Then, everyone was ordered out of the coach. Gentlemen would be asked to toss their watches and money into the robber's hat, while in some instances ladies might be allowed to keep their jewels. Next taken would be the mail itself before the robbers would gallop off for their homes in the hills.

A COLLEGE IS REROUTED

When a driver hit a rut in the road—if he had time and his wits about him—one remedy he might try was to loudly advise his passengers "lean to the right!" if he thought the coach was about to tip over to the left or "lean to the left!" should he anticipate a fall in the other direction—thus encouraging the passengers' active participation in road safety. But even with quick wits and cooperation, upsets could not always be avoided, and some passengers got very upset indeed.

Today, Randolph-Macon College sits comfortably just off a railway line a little north of Richmond in Ashland. It might not be there except for one truly terrible stagecoach ride, because it used to be in a completely different part of the state. Randolph-Macon College was originally built in 1830 in Boydton, Virginia, near the North Carolina border. It was named for the aforementioned sometimes testy soul of John Randolph of Roanoke and a North Carolina statesman, Nathaniel Macon. Boydton, too, sat on a railroad line, but it was a less prominent one that was destroyed in the Civil War and not rebuilt, so stagecoaches were the way to reach it.

According to *Lost Communities of Virginia*, after the Civil War, the college's trustees were to meet in Boydton to decide the fate of the far-flung campus. Unfortunately, the stagecoach in which the trustees rode was traveling through rain and the resulting mud. The coach hit a rut in the road, throwing the passengers into the muck. After such a disheartening experience, the trustees voted to move the school many miles away to Ashland, which was adjacent to a working rail line. In Boydton, you can still see the remains of the original college's stately buildings, doomed by a rut in the road and a spell of rainy weather.

HE HAD A WORD FOR IT

Charles Dickens wasn't the only literary lion to experience the unique challenges of an extended Virginia stagecoach ride. Noah Webster, whose name is still emblazoned on some of the best-regarded dictionaries, had decided to go on an author tour, making speeches and selling his marvelous lexicon. The year was 1785, and Noah Webster cursed all stage waggons. That is what he wrote in his diary on May 18, and he meant it.

Unfortunately for Webster, stage waggons factored as a key component of his travel plans. Sadly, they proved unreliable, unpredictable and downright dangerous. The stage waggon he took from Baltimore to Alexandria, Virginia, overturned, forcing him back to his starting point. So he hired a horse and rode fifty miles in a day to make it to Alexandria. Webster was in the midst of travels that took him from Connecticut to South Carolina. His three-volume reference set included a grammar book, speller and book of practice readings. Ultimately, Webster devised what would become a truly popular textbook that relied on American English with examples that used local places and names that would be familiar to the inhabitants of the newly minted country.

Horseback was Webster's preferred transport, but sometimes he did go by stage waggon, shipping the majority of his inventory aboard the plentiful sloops that conveyed people and goods around the coasts. Whether he rode on horseback or on a cursed stage waggon, Webster would have largely been using the main roads that connected one town to another. On those occasions when he had a horse, the inns and taverns were prepared to house them both, and it was common for a person starting a long trip to buy a horse at the beginning and sell it at the end or, as Webster sometimes did, hire a horse from a livery stable attached to or near the inn, one after another, until the destination was reached.

Webster had a good reputation, so in addition to sometimes spending the night at an inn, he frequently stayed with friends and acquaintances. He was a guest at Mount Vernon and characteristically advised George Washington to hire an American tutor for his step-grandchildren rather than seeking one abroad.

His book tour was a great success. For a fee, he began giving public lectures to larger and larger crowds on the importance of developing their new country's own language rather than continuing to copy the British forms. American English had acquired different words—twelve thousand of them by the 1828 edition of his *American Dictionary of the English Language*—and the cursed "waggon" had Americanized itself to "wagon" just as the more streamlined stagecoach was rising in popularity.

A STAGECOACH TRIP IN 1870
OVER THE MIDLAND TRAIL

Even when things went right, with no upsets or robberies, a stagecoach trip was something to be endured. In nearly one hundred years since Webster made his trip, things had not improved very much for stagecoach passengers—at least not by 1870. The following adventure was set down in *Tales and Trails from the "Fayette Tribune."* In 1926, Thomas E. Jeffries of Charleston, West Virginia, wrote to the *Daily Mail* telling some of his experiences in traveling on the old stagecoaches. There were no pleasures in this sort of trip, he declared, and emphasized that travel by this method was slow.

"They had lost the habit of traveling fast in 1870," he said.

> *While the C&O was under construction it was the custom to send monthly estimates of the work done to the Charleston [West Virginia] office where they were gone over, made into a package and sent to Richmond by a special messenger, and after they were gone over and checked, returned to Charleston by the same men, the money to meet them being sent by express.*
>
> *My pay as rodman at that time was $1.50 per day, and as the pay of this messenger was $2.50 a day and expenses, I thought I had a soft snap when I got this extra job. I made only one round trip.*
>
> *The stage left the Kanawha house corner of Kanawha and Summers streets in Charleston at 4 a.m. I had a friend named Charley Kuper, who was riding a fine horse to some little town in Virginia, leaving here at the same time as the stage. Charley passed out of sight in the darkness before we reached Hale St. It was in October, and the roads were of as perfect condition as they could be. We changed horses at the Ten Mile House opposite Marmet, at Bowmans and at Kanawha Falls. When we drove up to the hotel at the Falls at 2 p.m. where we had dinner, Charley was just leaving, having had his dinner, fed and rested his horse for an hour. We had half an hour for dinner, and then started east again, driving all night without stopping for supper. We stopped for breakfast on top of Big Sewell, and were just coming out when Charley rode up, he having slept at least part of the night at a farm house. We drove into White Sulphur at 2 p.m., 110 miles in 34 hours, or a little over 3 miles an hour. Some speed at that.*
>
> *I was in Richmond three days. Leaving by rail for White Sulphur. There was no such thing as an air brake and continuing couplers, or sleepers, and every time the train started or stopped, you felt like your head was going to be jerked off. I was just thinking of making some kind of a bed with*

two seats when the train stopped at a little town, and Charley got aboard with a basket of peaches. So we ate peaches and smoked all night, arriving at White Sulphur after dinner. We did not register anywhere, as we were leaving early in the morning and were not feeling any too good. (There seems to be a limit to the number of peaches you can eat in one night.)

Charles bought a bottle of brandy and we both took a drink and felt some better. There was a masquerade ball on at the White and we hung around and watched the pretty girls dance, and were still hanging around at 4 am when the stage started.

We drove all that day and all night except when we stopped for meals and to change horses. At times the driver would stop at a spring and all hands get out and get a drink of water. We sometimes wished the springs were closer together. I had been riding with the driver most of the time, because the effort to keep from being thrown off kept me awake, but just as we started down the divide, and I was about to go crazy for want of sleep, I got down and entered the coach. Charley had preempted the back seat and appeared to be asleep or drunk, so I rolled him off the seat onto the floor and doubled up in the seat. Were you ever tossed up in a blanket? Well, that's just how it felt except when you came down you seemed to hit every bone in your body at the same time. As Charley still slept on, I concluded he was drunk. We reached Charleston between 4 and 5 in the afternoon—36 hours out from White Sulphur—110 miles—figure it out for yourself.

I delivered the package of estimates and got home at 5 p.m. Ate my supper, went to bed, and was asleep when I hit the bed. I awoke in the morning very much refreshed, but hungry. The sun was shining brightly but everything was still. I thought it must be very early, but got up anyway, thinking I could find something to eat. When I got down stairs, I found my mother was up and having heard me she was putting my breakfast on the table. I said, "Mother, how come you to have vegetables for breakfast?" "This is dinner," she said, "It's nearly 2 o'clock." I had slept nearly 20 hours without a break. That was the last time I took the trip.

If any old timer tells you about the pleasures of a trip on the stage, don't believe him, as you can't pack the same amount of discomfort in the same length of time in any other way. When the roads were on the level you traveled in a cloud of dust, and when you were on the hills, there was more rocks in the road than you could count, and the driver hit every one of them. There were three seats, the front and rear ones had firm backs, and the people in the middle seat had to depend on a broad strap or leather fastened to the sides of the coach, and while all were more or less scrambled, the ones on the middle seat were double scrambled.

XI
THE PEOPLE WHO MADE STAGECOACHES WORK

CHICKEN PUDDING, A FAVOURITE VIRGINIA DISH

BEAT ten eggs very light, add to them a quart of rich milk, with a quarter of a pound of butter melted, and some pepper and salt; stir in as much flour as will make a thin good batter; take four young chickens, and after cleaning them nicely, cut off the legs, wings, &c. put. them all in a sauce pan, with some salt and water, and a bundle of thyme and parsley, boil them till nearly done, then take the chicken from the water and put it in the batter, pour it in a deep dish, and bake it; send nice white gravy in a boat.

Stagecoach Days and Stagecoach Kings lists some of the personnel and places needed to run a successful stage line.

On a well-established line, a conductor usually rode with the driver—who might also be called a reinsman or a whip—and collected fares, took care of passengers and had charge of the mail. As the stagecoach neared the station, the conductor might blow a stage horn to alert passengers of their imminent arrival.

Besides these, a stagecoach line also provided work for a number of other people. A well-equipped stagecoach stop would need an ostler and stable hands to look after the horses and keep a relay team of horses ready to relieve the tired ones coming in off the road. A stagecoach stop that only supplied a change of horses was called a swing station.

An inn at a "home station" would provide rest for the weary and food for the hungry. Nearby might be a blacksmith to tend to any loose horseshoes and a harness-maker and wheelwright for repairing or replacing equipment.

A joiner would make any repairs of the inside woodwork, such as the doors and molding. All of those things might be clustered around a central building and owned by an extended family, but in larger towns, there might be more than one tavern, a bevy of stores to tempt travelers, a racetrack, courthouses, a mill and other practical proofs of commerce.

According to Colonial Williamsburg's "Stage Waggons and Coaches," the Woolfolk family papers, held at William & Mary's Swem Library, describe the accounts of their stage line in the late eighteenth century. The line ran from the Cross Roads, near Bowling Green in Caroline County, Virginia, to Portsmouth, Virginia, by way of Richmond, Petersburg and Suffolk.

It had quite a few expenses, most of them relating to feed for horses. The teams consumed different kinds—corn, oats, bran and hay. The wages paid out were mostly for the drivers, but some were for people who manned stations along the route. There were also repair costs for the wagons and horses' harness. During the time period covered by the account books, about twelve horses were purchased, with prices ranging from six to twenty-six pounds. Both feed and horses might be bought over time rather than paid in full when purchased. Harness in 1808 cost ten pounds per set.

THE DRIVERS

The stagecoach driver sat in his box like a king on his throne. His twelve-foot whip was held aslant in his right hand, while with his left hand he controlled four sets of "ribbons" or reins. Beside him sat the conductor ready to sound a note of warning on the glittering stagehorn if any vehicle did not pull aside to let the mail express dash through.

—Stagecoach Days and Stagecoach Kings

American stagecoach drivers, as noted by European travelers, were not servile in their demeanor. Their jobs were obviously difficult, as they had to contend with foul weather, foul-tempered passengers and rough roads and were expected to control four thousand pounds of not always cooperative horseflesh traveling at high speeds with two sets of "ribbons" and a whip, sometimes in the middle of a moonless night. They were in complete command of their passengers. If they thought a hill too steep for their horses to climb, passengers would be asked to get out to lighten the load. If a wheel became stuck in the mire, the able-bodied would need to get out and push. And if part of the coach happened to break, they might be asked to look the other way while a portion of a farmer's fence was rigged as a replacement.

As part of their pay, drivers' expenses for food and board at stage stops were covered. However, unlike their British counterparts, they did not generally accept tips or gratuities, making them far less likely to adopt anything akin to a servant's demeanor. Drivers were regarded as responsible, brave and independent, more like the captain of a ship than a lackey, and they took their responsibilities seriously.

Englishman Richard Parkinson (1748–1815), an agricultural specialist who visited Mount Vernon, wrote in his book *A Tour of America in 1798, 1799 and 1800*:

> *The drivers of coaches (Stage Waggons) are in general sober men, and it is not usual for the passengers to give the coachman money at the end of the stage, as in England. Indeed he considers himself equal to any one, and seemingly, it would be an offense to offer him money. He will drink a glass with you as a companion, but in no other way. The coachmen drive but one stage, from fourteen to twenty miles, and take care of their own horses, which is one cause of their good appearance.*

He had less kind things to say about George Washington's and other American farmers' practices.

The rides those sober drivers gave were rarely dull. In 1838, traveling phrenologist (one who thought the shape of the skull was directly related to character) George Combe observed: "The youth who drove us ascended the numerous hills which we traversed very leisurely, but dashed down the other side with extraordinary rapidity."

Mechanical brakes hadn't been invented yet, so if such a precaution was wanted, it was necessary to stop the coach and attach a mechanical drag to slow down on a rapid descent. A lot of drivers simply didn't bother with it, preferring to run their horses at full-tilt. As set down in Holmes's *Stagecoach East*, a passenger on a coach in the long and winding Alleghenies observed:

> *The practice is for the team to be put on a run the moment they gain the summit of a hill, and if all things hold out, this is kept up until the bottom is reached: the horses are excellent, and rarely fail. On my asking the coachman,—by whom I rode as much as possible,—what he did in the event the wheel-horse coming down in a steep pass, he replied 'Why, I*

"A Mountain Stage." *Author's collection.*

keep driving ahead, and drag him along.'—an accident which he assured me had occurred more than once to himself when the roads were encrusted with ice and snow.

Drivers famous for their skill were called "crack" reinsmen and were often given the honorary title of captain out of respect, whether or not they had seen military service. According to *Stagecoach Days and Stagecoach Kings*, the twelve-foot whips were more loud and symbolic than employed to inflict pain. Depending on his preference, a driver might dress casually or handsomely, but in cold weather, he would certainly dress warmly.

In the western reaches of Virginia, the stagecoach drivers were celebrated as remarkable characters. According to *Tales and Trails from the "Fayette Tribune,"* two well-known drivers in the days just before the Civil War were Jack Wines and John Leonard. Local humorists used to say that Leonard's horn seemed to speak the words "Jack Wines! Jack Wines! Hook up your horses, we are coming now" when approaching a station where Wines was to take his place.

Wines and Leonard were driving in the mountains of western Virginia, a place notorious for stage accidents, and Route 60 still has remarkable curves and sudden drops in elevation. It was worse before. *The Gazetteer of*

Virginia in 1835 gave a vivid description of the perils that beset one coming over the mountains: "I have been credibly exposed to imminent peril. At one of the narrow defiles the stage with eight passengers and driver, rolled down a steep declivity of fifty feet, and although the stage turned three somersaults and was actually shattered to fragments—neither horses or passengers suffered material injury."

Whether this was due to the skill of the driver or Divine Providence was no doubt a matter of debate. Fortunately, there was likely a station within ten miles of the upset.

JAMES ISAACS

Not every well-regarded stagecoach driver was a white man. A 2010 article in the Charlottesville *Daily Progress* went back in time to tell the story of James "Jinks" Isaacs, a former slave who drove the stage on routes from Richmond to Staunton for forty years. Before Emancipation, he had been owned by William Farish, a Baptist minister who ran a well-known stage line and the still-standing Farish House Hotel at 300 Court Square in Charlottesville. James Isaacs continued to drive for a decade after the Civil War as a free man until his death.

At Isaacs's passing in 1876, Reverend Robert Steele's elegy at the African Methodist Episcopal church in Staunton stressed his "high character" and moral constitution as well as his ability to drive a team of four-in-hand. His routes involved fording two potentially dangerous rivers as well as numerous streams.

James Isaacs was very much the master of his stagecoach. Should a male passenger dare to show less than chivalrous behavior to any female, his eulogy revealed that he was quite prepared to leave the offender on the side of the road. When he died, his life was written up in both the Staunton and Charlottesville papers, and citizens black and white attended his funeral to show their respect.

A WOMAN'S TOUCH...ON THE REINS

The most likely job for women in the world of stagecoaches was providing a place to sleep and meals to eat at a tavern or inn. Traditionally, a widow would have the skills of a cook and housekeeper—and she might also be in possession of a house that could be adapted to provide hospitality for travelers. Also, the widow of an established tavern keeper, such as Mrs. Boswell, might keep the family business going for years after her husband's death.

But there was at least one woman stagecoach driver in Virginia.

"Old Moll" Tate drove the night stage from Abingdon to Blountville for several years. She took up driving to support her child after her husband and other children died from a plague. An extraordinary woman, she had an extraordinary start, with fourteen given names—one for each of the women who attended her birth and one for each of her aunts: Mary Melzeeda Susan Elizabeth Cynthia Parnintha Sarah Adeline Rosey Daisy Laura Lucretia Louisa Jane. She went by Mary, which soon became Moll and eventually Old Moll during her stagecoach days. According to a lively account in *Pioneers in Paradise*, she was born into the Gragg family in the vicinity of Washington County, Virginia, and her presence was remembered long after her passing.

Moll had been working as a field hand to make ends meet, but one of her employers, knowing how well she could handle a team of workhorses, joked that she should consider taking up driving the stagecoach. That sounded like a fine idea to her, so she did it and became a respected and beloved institution in her community.

Cracking her whip over her team, she would drive them through the night if need be and sleep on hard wooden floors between shifts if that was all there was. After having her mail stolen once, she rigged a dummy bag to foist on any would-be robbers. Old Moll was also a crack shot, and it was said she could knock out a squirrel's eye at fifty yards. She had extraordinary night vision, which was well, for on a windy night in 1859, she stopped the coach in time to avoid a tree in the road. When she was out of the coach and about to oversee the task of getting the tree cut up and away from the thoroughfare, three masked and armed robbers emerged from the woods. They did succeed in taking both the mail and the passengers' money, but Old Moll swore revenge.

As soon as she could, she drove into town sounding the emergency signal and gathered the sheriff and his posse. The robbers, flush with stolen money and readily spending it, were apprehended in a neighboring town. That did not satisfy Old Moll, though, and she is said to have descended upon the jail, informing the sheriff and the jailer that she intended to "whip them breeches off them devils" who had the effrontery to rob her stage and her passengers. The sheriff agreed, and she very nearly did just that. The rest of her story can be found in *Pioneers in Paradise*, which has marvelous descriptions of what stage drivers and passengers experienced in the mid-1800s in that part of Virginia, many based on first-hand accounts.

Old Moll's part in the stagecoach age was being a driver, doing a difficult job well night after night with skill, bravery and compassion. She was an extraordinary but typically uneducated woman, not the sort to socialize with legislators and make the rules—and the routes—upon which those stages ran.

"EXTRA BILLY" IN THE SPOTLIGHT

William Smith, representative from Virginia to the Thirty-Fifth Congress, 1859. *Photograph by Julian Vannerson, courtesy of the Library of Congress.*

Virginia had its own "stagecoach kings" who were the businessmen behind it all. Perhaps the most famous of them was William Smith (1797–1887). Given the contract to carry the mail in his coaches, he was nicknamed "Extra Billy" for all the extra routes he tacked onto the regular lines. They surely gave more convenience to the customers just as they increased Extra Billy's income, for Congress was obliged to pay for those extra runs.

Eventually, Extra Billy would become a state governor—twice—and he also served as a major general in the Confederate army during the Civil War, where he was the oldest Southern general to hold a field command. A recent biography, *Confederate General William "Extra Billy" Smith: From Virginia's Statehouse to Gettysburg Scapegoat*, details much of his wartime career. Born at Marengo in King George County, just down the King's Highway (Route 3) from Fredericksburg, William Smith trained to be a lawyer after attending private schools in Virginia and Connecticut and settled in Culpeper. His first venture into stage lines was a relatively short run between Culpeper and Fairfax. In 1827, he was granted the U.S. government's permission to start a major stagecoach line between Washington, D.C., and Milledgeville, then the capital of Georgia. Those extra fees he was granted for spur routes, including connecting steamboat lines, came to public light when the Post Office Department, whose seal featured a post rider, was investigated.

William's father, Colonel Caleb Smith, served several terms in the Virginia General Assembly, so it is not surprising that William, too, should become a representative, and he was politically active in the antebellum period, during the war itself, and afterward, up to the year of his death. But his was not to be a peaceful tenure.

In journalist Benjamin Perley Poore's *Reminiscences*, he recalls watching an elderly Extra Billy engage Poore's editor at the *Evening Star*, a Mr. Wallach, in an argument on Pennsylvania Avenue. It soon went from harsh name-calling to wrestling. Then the elderly Extra Billy

> *threw Wallach heavily to the sidewalk. Sitting on his prostrate foe, Smith began to pummel him, but at first blow Wallach got one of his antagonist's thumbs in his mouth where he held it as if it were in a vise. Smith roared, "Let go my thumb! You are eating it to the bone!" Just then up came Mr. Keitt, of South Carolina, and Mr. Bocock, of Virginia, who went to the rescue of Smith, Keitt saying: "This is no way for gentlemen to settle their disputes," as he forced Wallach's jaws apart, to release the "chawed-up" thumb. Wallach was uninjured, but for several weeks he went heavily armed, expecting that Smith would attack him.*

Feisty Extra Billy Smith still has his admirers to this day. Extra Billy's Smokehouse and Brewery in the Richmond area gives another explanation for its namesake's nickname: he always put in "extra" effort in whatever he undertook. No doubt that was true as well.

XII

HEADING SOUTH

TO MAKE DROP BISCUIT

BEAT eight eggs very light, add to them twelve ounces of flour, and one pound of sugar; when perfectly light, drop them on tin sheets, and bake them in a quick oven.

MACON TAVERN

Heading southward, the scenery was often rural, with towns few and far between. Taverns and inns, with their accompanying facilities for horses, were still needed for the stages, so they might be built at crossroads. Macon Tavern, built at a crossroads leading to Tobaccoville, Scottsville and Amelia, was rather small, with only one bedroom upstairs, three rooms on the first floor and a basement containing the kitchen, but it was a well-known gathering spot for local farmers traveling to market for generations. In time, it became a private residence. A portion of it is still standing today.

According to "French Place Names in Virginia," Macon, in Powhatan County, was founded in 1753 by Henry Macon, a descendant of William Macon, whose patent for land there was granted as early as 1729. William's father, Gideon, was a Huguenot who settled in New Kent County in the seventeenth century. The Huguenots were French Protestants, many of whom fled their home country when Louis XIV revoked the Edict of Nantes in 1685. The edict had provided a measure of protection and tolerance for the religious dissenters. Persecution, including massacres, followed its revocation, and many Huguenots, such as Macon, made their way to the American colonies.

Sublett's was another tavern owned by Huguenot descendants in Powhatan County. William Sublett established the post office there in 1819. The name in the original French was likely either Soblet or Sobler, as immigrants with those names were known in the area. Manakin Town, named for the Indian tribe that formerly lived there, was a well-known Huguenot settlement in Goochland County, northeast of Richmond.

PRIME REAL ESTATE AT THE STATE CAPITAL

Of course, Richmond, being located on the James River, was a logical place for stagecoaches and their associated taverns, particularly in the days before railway lines made such an impact on economic and settlement patterns.

One of Richmond's noted taverns was the Swan, at the corner of Broad and Ninth Streets. In its early days, it was kept by Major John Moss, who was likely a Revolutionary War officer. Notable guests included Thomas Jefferson and a certain writer of the macabre: Edgar Allan Poe stopped here on his last visit to Richmond.

John G. Mitchell was the aggressive editor of the *Richmond Planet*. *Courtesy of the New York Public Library Digital Collections.*

In 1888, black newspaper editor and publisher John Mitchell Jr. moved his landmark, albeit struggling, *Richmond Planet* operations to an office in the Swan's basement. The Swan was built in the late 1780s and stood on its corner until 1904, when it was demolished. Interestingly, its place was later taken by the Richmond Trailways bus station, which made sense as it was a very central location. But that too was demolished to make way for the Library of Virginia in 1997. The library takes up an entire block, has its own garage and is an excellent place to research stagecoaches, taverns, early newspapers and so much more about the state's past.

And where might early travelers be going from the Swan? A road runs out to the Tidewater area from Richmond to Gloucester. There, today's visitors

Composing room of the *Planet*, Richmond, Virginia, ca. 1899. *Courtesy of the Library of Congress.*

can go to the Gloucester Museum of History, also known as the Botetourt Building. Before it was the Botetourt Building, it was the Botetourt Hotel, and before it took that name, it was built in the late eighteenth century as a roadside tavern known as John New's Ordinary. It is one of the largest and one of the few brick taverns surviving from the period. The museum is concerned with many aspects of local history and is managed by Gloucester County.

AT OLD YORKTOWN

Yorktown, Virginia, site of the last battle of the Revolutionary War, not surprisingly had its share of taverns. Today, you can see another Swan Tavern—this one reconstructed—on the National Park Service property. The original Swan Tavern was built by 1722 and for 130 years, until 1852, was the leading hostelry at Yorktown. Located at the corner of Main and

Swan Tavern, main building, Yorktown, Virginia, 1933. *Courtesy of the Historic American Buildings Survey, Library of Congress.*

Ballard Streets, it was a gathering place for seafarers (Yorktown was an important port), tobacco traders, merchants and many others.

According to Yorktown's Main Street Historic Resource Study by the National Park Service, in the 1820s, this was another case where the widow of a tavern keeper continued the family business—if she had a proper license of course. It read in part:

> *If therefore the said Lucy Wills doth constantly find and provide in her said Ordinary good wholesome and clean lodging and diet for Travellers and Stableage, fodder and provender on pasterage and provender as the season shall require for their horses, until the next May term of the County of York, and shall not suffer or permit any unlawful gaming in her house nor suffer any person to tipple and drink more than is necessary then the above obligation is void or else to remain in full force and virtue.*

Yorktown's Swan Tavern closed in 1852 and was demolished in the course of the Civil War in 1863. The National Park Service reconstructed it in 1934.

Another building that was later used as a tavern in Yorktown, Somerwell House—also known as Old English Tavern, the Yorktown Hotel and Dawson's Hotel—was still in use as a hotel when the Park Service took it over for administration and dormitory housing for staff in the 1930s.

XIII
ROADS WEST

BUCKWHEAT CAKES

Put a large spoonful of yeast and a little salt, into a quart of buckwheat meal; make it into a batter with cold water; let it rise well, and bake it on a griddle—it turns sour very quickly, if it be allowed to stand any time after it has risen.

The roads west into the Shenandoah Valley ran along the limestone beds that naturally lay there, deposited many thousands of years ago when a sea overlaid the land. The resulting lime-rich soil benefitted agriculture in the valley, so much so that its crop yields were often twice that of the state as a whole, according to *The Great Valley Road of Virginia*. Besides the agricultural industry, the tourism industry would also benefit, for limestone is semipermeable and resulted in both the popular springs resorts and natural wonders, such as Luray and Shenandoah Caverns.

BETTER ROADS MEAN BETTER BUSINESS

But to make money from all that agriculture, farmers would need roads—good roads—to get their produce to market. Later on, railways would be the preferred mode of transport, but until that day, there must be long stretches of good roads in place. By the 1760s, the triple strain on resources made by industrialization, population increases and feeding the armies for the wars in Europe led to a great increase in the demand for flour, which wound its profitable way down the wagon roads of the Shenandoah and into port cities in the Tidewater region of Virginia.

The culture that developed in the Shenandoah Valley was much less homogenous than that of the Tidewater region. The Tidewater landowners were mainly English, but heading west, a traveler would see other influences. Quite striking were the large groups of German-speaking peoples, many of whom had taken the Great Valley Road from Pennsylvania to western Virginia. These settlers maintained their own language to the point that a number of German-language newspapers were printed in the Shenandoan Valley. Their agriculture was different, too, with less tobacco being grown. Instead, there was more of a concentration on livestock and grain.

In 1820, Frederick County, Virginia, was the number one flour producer in the state, but it was far away from a port, emphasizing again the need to develop good roads for commerce. Once the roads were well established, businesses—including stagecoaches and taverns—began to thrive in their wake.

Building new roads involved a lot of work and expense. First, there had to be an agreement to build the road. That happened on the political level, usually among well-educated men with well-lined pockets. Then came the surveying—a tedious and somewhat dangerous proposition. Once the surveying was finished, it was necessary to map possible routes and determine the best one. Then there was the matter of building and financing the road. Better roads cost more money, so sometimes economies were made that might spell trouble for travelers later on. But in time, better roads were built, and some of those were more or less self-financed turnpikes. For a stagecoach to take a turnpike, each passenger as well as the driver was expected to pay a fee at various points along the way.

THE VALLEY TURNPIKE

In 1834, the Valley Turnpike Company was incorporated. It was authorized to build a seventy-odd-mile stretch of turnpike from Winchester to Harrisonburg and was empowered by its charter to use as much of "the old stage road" as was feasible. In 1837, a second stretch of macadamized turnpike to link Harrisonburg and Staunton was begun. Although the turnpike was still under construction when Claudius Crozet completed his map of the state's internal improvements, it was clear the turnpike was going to be important. Macadamization to make roads a better surface for travel was still underway in 1840 when an upper valley resident noted, "They have got the Macadamized road nearly completed from Staunton to Winchester."

Before the railroads were established, these turnpikes guaranteed the flow of trade and travelers, leading to the state's prosperity. The center of each rural community along the way would often be a mill—a place where people could go to grind their corn or wheat. As bread was considered "the staff of life," it only made sense that the place of its flour milling would be the center of a village's life.

OVER THE MOUNTAINS ON THE JAMES RIVER PIKE

According to *Tales and Trails from the Fayette Tribune*, the first stage line to operate between Lewisburg and Charleston, later West Virginia's state capital, began in 1827. Only one trip was made each week, and the fare was the considerable sum (for the time) of seven dollars. Preference was given in the order in which passengers registered for the seats, but passengers traveling by steamboats counting on a connection to a stage line were given first preference. If there was still room in or on top of the coach, the driver might pick up some more fares along the road. Passengers were allowed twenty pounds of baggage carried for free on the stage. More might be carried at the option of the driver and charged at the rate of four dollars per hundred pounds for one hundred miles. Eventually, the coaches were making the trip several times a week, with some advertising a rest on Sunday.

As to the comfort of this mode of travel, the *Gazetteer of Virginia* in 1835, as relayed in *Tales and Trails*, gives a vivid description of the perils that beset one coming over the mountains—with possible peril from an irritable tavern keeper:

> *To accommodate the increasing travel, better houses of entertainment were provided at regular intervals along the road. These taverns actually had great open fire-place in the tap room, that one reads about in fiction, and steaming drinks were served to cold travelers who harped about it. Brawling was rare among the better class of patrons, and ministers took a glass for*

"the stomach's sake." A glass of port often lent color to the feminine cheek and to fortify one against a cold ride on the coach. Should a guest become rude while partaking of the hospitality of the tavern, he found the owner was able to preserve order. At one tavern along this road a stage passenger once became boisterous at the dinner table. The tavern keeper was a rough, genial soul, but possessed with a terrible temper when peeved. He was also a great bear hunter, and on this particular day he stalked into the dining room dressed in buck-skin shirt, coon-skin cap and moccasins, to the amusement of the boisterous party, who began to make remarks to the diners about his costume. The tavern keeper struck him with a loaf of bread, leaped over the table, seized him and gouged his eye out. Stamping his moccasin in the blood of the unfortunate man, he made the imprint of his foot on the wall, so as he explained that all who followed OLD JAMES RIVER PIKE after could see he was able to take care of his own house.

ENTERPRISE AND INVENTIVENESS AT STEELE'S TAVERN

Taverns were places where the community gathered to learn what was new. In 1831, local lad Cyrus McCormick demonstrated a new machine he had invented—the first practical grain reaper. He demonstrated it in a field of oats owned by tavern keeper John Steele. John Steele's father, David, was a Revolutionary War veteran. He and his young wife provided hospitality to travelers along Route 11. When the stagecoaches started running on the road, they needed a place to change horses and refresh themselves, which they did at Steele's Tavern in Augusta County.

A small village grew up around the tavern, with a store, blacksmith's shop, post office, town hall, church, flour mills, cooper shop and, eventually, a two-

The McCormick reaper of 1847.
Courtesy of the New York Public Library Digital Collections.

room schoolhouse. It was in the tavern's blacksmith shop that young Cyrus worked out the particulars of his mechanical reaper, building on the work of his father, also an inventor, and with the help of a slave named Jo Anderson. Cyrus McCormick patented the reaper in 1834. He continued to improve the design and make them individually until after his father's death, when he and his brother moved to Chicago to start producing them in a factory.

It is said that this invention eventually brought on the mechanization of agriculture. Today, historic McCormick Farm is home to the Shenandoah Valley Agricultural Research and Extension Center. Nearby, Steele's Tavern Manor Bed & Breakfast, built in 1916 to house Steele family descendants, continues to extend hospitality to visitors.

XIV
THE CIVIL WAR

TO FRY SLICED POTATOS

Peel large potatos, slice them about a quarter of an inch thick, or cut them in shavings round and round, as you would peel a lemon; dry them well in a clean cloth, and fry them in lard or dripping. Take care that your fat and frying-pan are quite clean; put it on a quick fire, watch it, and as soon as the lard boils and is still, put in the slices of potatos, and keep moving them till they are crisp; take them up, and lay them to drain on a sieve; send them up with very little salt sprinkled on them.

THE WAR BEGINS

No longer standing, Taylor's Tavern in Falls Church faced the Alexandria–Leesburg Pike and was quite the place to sojourn in its day. A two-story tavern on fifty-six acres with verandas, it was built by William Taylor about 1800. It became militarily important during the Civil War and was one of the first places the North and South faced each other. It was also the site of the first aerial reconnaissance mission in the United States—by balloon flight—on June 24, 1861, a little less than a month before the Battle of First Manassas. The name of the balloon was the *Enterprise*. In *History of the Seventeenth Virginia, C.S.A.*, the author George Wise recalled: "Numbers of amusing incidents, various hair-breadth escapes, occurred to those on duty

Soldiers standing in front of Taylor's Tavern near Falls Church, Virginia, 1861–65. *Courtesy of the Library of Congress.*

in that vicinity: and the minds of many on perusing these pages will revert to the early morning fights between the pickets of the enemy and themselves, over the little peach orchard and rich gardens below Taylor's tavern."

Today, the tavern's site is marked by Fort Taylor Park.

At still-standing Old Stone House in Manassas, history records a woman named Mary "Polly" Clark, who had a wagon stand at the tollgate to provide food and drink to travelers. The Old Stone House itself seems to have been built in 1848 by Thomas O. Carter, the son of Polly Clark. It was sold out of the family in 1850. Not surprisingly, its sturdy walls became a Union hospital during the Battle of First Manassas, with wounded even being placed on the dirt floor of the cellar. According to a contemporary account, one inexperienced surgeon was left to tend thirty-two wounded men. Many did not live. As the tide of battle turned, the building fell into Confederate hands and continued to be used as a makeshift hospital.

In August 1862, the Old Stone House was used as a Union hospital again, and two soldiers carved their names in the floorboards on the second story. One would survive the war and live into the next century. The other would not survive the year.

After the war, the house went back to its original purpose as a tollhouse, and its profits enabled the owners to maintain it during the later 1800s. Sold to the federal government in 1949, the Old Stone House is now often included on interpreted tours of the Manassas Battlefield.

Naturally talk in the taverns was about the war. Built around 1790, Old Birds Nest Tavern (or Birdsnest) would have accommodated both stagecoach passengers and those crossing the Chesapeake Bay by ferry.

Old Birds Nest Tavern, Marionville, Northampton County, Virginia, ca. 1930. *Photograph by Frances Benjamin Johnston, courtesy of the Carnegie Survey of the Architecture of the South, Library of Congress.*

According to information with its photograph at the Library of Congress, this Northampton County landmark was known as a sailor's tavern.

In late 1861, David Nottingham Bull (or Bool) got drunk at Birdsnest Tavern and started speaking against slavery, saying that owners had no right to consider their slaves as property. He was convicted of a misdemeanor and sentenced to three months in jail, but he was freed by Union troops, who released him and gave him charge of the lighthouse on Hog Island.

As fighting spread across the Old Dominion and newly established West Virginia, it took its toll on the small ordinaries and inns that could not withstand the shock of being on the battlefield. Some of the well-established ones, such as Tyree Tavern, became troop headquarters for either side—and therefore potential military targets.

SOMBER REFLECTIONS

John Sergeant Wise (1846–1913), the son of Virginia governor Henry Wise, gives a moving, descriptive account of how it was in the small town of Rocky Mount, Virginia, in 1862, and the importance of the stagecoach connection during the early years of the war:

> *The tavern porch was the rallying-point of the town: hither all news came; here all news was discussed; hence all news was disseminated. From this spot the daily stage departed in the morning. Here villagers and country folk assembled in the day and waited in the evening; and to this spot came the stage in the evening, bearing the mail, the war news, and such citizens as had been absent, visitors who drifted in, or soldiers returning sick, wounded, or on furlough.*

Supreme interest centred ever about the arrival or departure of the stage. In the foggy morning it appeared with its strong four-in-hand team, and took its place majestically in front of the old tavern. The porters rocked it as they dumped the baggage into the boot; the red-faced driver came forth from the breakfast-room with great self-importance. With his broad palm he wiped away the greasy remnants of his meal, lit his brier-root pipe, drew on his buckskin gloves, settled his slouched hat over his eyes, clambered to his seat upon the box, gathered his reins and whip, and cast a glance towards the post-office across the way; an aged man and a meek-eyed woman in simple garb slipped quietly into the rear seats, going perhaps on some sad mission under summons to a far-off hospital at the front; a dainty miss, with bonnet-box and bunch of flowers, kissed papa and mamma and took her place within, full of joyous anticipation, doubtless, for even in war times girls love to visit each other; a fat commissary, returning from his search in the back country for supplies, came forth, reeking with rum and tobacco, and swung up awkwardly to the seat beside the driver. Tom, Dick, and Harry, the new recruits bound for the front, proud in their new and misfit uniforms, seized mother, wife, sister, or sweetheart in their arms, kissed them, bade them have no fear, and scrambled lightly to the top. The lame and tardy postmaster hobbled forth at last, and threw his mail-pouch up to the dashboard. The coachman gave his warning cry of "all aboard"; the hostlers drew off the blankets, the long whip cracked its merry signal; with discord in each footfall at the start and concord as they caught the step, the horses pulled away; and the lumbering stage went grinding up the stony street, its horn signing its morning carol to those who were awake. As they disappeared over the hill-top, a last merry cry of parting came back from the bright boys on the stage-top, and the last they saw of home was the waving tokens of love from those they left behind....

By three or four o'clock, the tavern bar was liberally patronized. The recruiting-office had its full quota of young fellows inquiring about the terms of enlistment. The tavern porch was filled with people discussing war news, and the quartermaster down the street had more horses offered to him than he was authorized to buy....

The arrival of the stage not infrequently interrupted General Early's vigorous lectures. For half an hour or more before the event, the expectant throng would increase, and, as those who "brace" themselves for the crisis were there, as everywhere else, conversation grew louder and agitation greater as the time approached. Then the stage would heave in sight in the gloaming, and come rattling down the rough street, the horseshoes knocking fire from the flints. Before the smoking and jaded beasts had fairly stopped, loud inquiries would be made on all hands, of driver and passengers, for war news. Somebody would throw down the latest newspaper; somebody would mount a chair and read aloud; and, just as the news was encouraging or depressing, there would be cheering or silence. Then would come the rush for the mail to the post-office across the way.

The passengers, also, were a source of engrossing interest. There was young So-and-so, with his empty sleeve. A year ago he had left the place, and passed safely through all the earlier battles; but at Malvern Hill a grapeshot mutilated his left arm. Amputation followed, and now, after a long time in hospital, here he was, home again, pale and bleached, with an honorable discharge in his pocket, and maimed for life. And there, collapsed upon the rear seat, more dead than alive, too weak to move save with the assistance of friends, was a poor, wan fellow, whom nobody knew at first. How pitiful he seemed, as they helped him forth, his eyes sunken yet restless, his weak arms clinging about their necks, his limbs scarce able to support his weight, his frame racked by paroxysms of violent coughing! "Who is it?" passed from mouth to mouth. "Good God!" exclaimed some one at the whispered reply, "it can't be! That is not Jimmie Thomson. What! Not old man Hugh Thomson's son, down on Pig River? Why, man alive, I knew the boy well. He was one of the likeliest boys in this whole county. Surely, that ar skeleton can't be him!" But it was. The exposure of camp life had done for poor Jimmie what bullets had failed to do.

The above account was excerpted from the chapter "Among the Mountains" in John Sergeant Wise's book, *The End of an Era*; it was reprinted in *"Backsights:" Essays in Virginia Transportation History Volume One*.

A HOTEL TURNED HOSPITAL

Those traveling the Civil War trails should not miss the previously mentioned Exchange Hotel in Gordonsville, not many miles from Orange. Built to take advantage of the railroad station that came to town in the 1840s, its past as a Civil War hospital is very much part of its present as a Civil War medical museum. It took on its role as the Gordonsville Receiving Hospital in March 1862 and provided care for over seventy thousand men, including both Confederate and captured Union soldiers.

DIVIDED LOYALTIES IN THE WEST

Part of western Virginia, by now split away from its home state and called West Virginia, was an area of divided loyalties. The aforementioned Tyree's Tavern, also known as Halfway House, was located at Mountain Cove (now Ansted). Mountain Cove fielded its own Confederate home guard ("Mountain Cove Guards," Company B, Twenty-Second Regiment, Virginia Infantry), and tavern owner William Tyree himself became the captain of the same regiment's Company C, the "Fayetteville Rifles." The Twenty-Second Regiment was commanded by George S. Patton Sr., the grandfather of the famed World War II general who carried his name.

SHE STOOD HER GROUND

A second tavern owned by the Tyree family, about seventeen miles east of Halfway House, was called Old Stone Tavern or Tyree Stone Tavern in Fayette County. In its heyday, it featured a hewn log stable fifty feet long by thirty feet wide and thirty feet high.

According to an account set down by "an unknown Confederate soldier" and printed in Tim McKinney's *The Civil War in Fayette County*, the innkeeper did not take kindly to having her livestock and garden looted by Federal troops:

> *We pursued the enemy as far as Mr. Tyree's, some eight miles. Mrs. Tyree is quite a favorite with our army. Though both her sons are volunteers, and her husband one of our most reliable scouts, she positively refused to flee from her home on the approach of the enemy. She penned her chickens, hogs, and cattle under her own eye, and armed with nothing but a single gun and a brave spirit, she was determined to stand her ground and protect herself and property. When the enemy approached, they pitched into her chicken coop and garden and she pitched into them. With a pitchfork she ran them out of her house, and returning to the other side of her house, she found several Hessians cutting her cabbage and bearing them off. Snatching up her gun and leveling it at them, they dropped their plunder and retreated in more than double quick time. The circumstances not only occasioned great diversion among the army, but her heroic conduct satisfied them that she could only be robbed by being killed, and they never after troubled anything*

she had by violence. Mrs. Tyree is a fine lady, of good character, and extraordinary will and nerve. She keeps one of the best hotels in western Virginia, and it is a favorite resort of all travelers.

The Kanawha Valley Campaign did not go well for the Confederacy, and the soldiers of the Twenty-Second eventually fell in for battles in the eastern part of the state.

Historic Inns of Southern West Virginia, by Ed Robinson, gives many examples of western Virginia inns that were used by armies during the war, including Miller Tavern (built in 1830) at Gauley Bridge in Fayette County, which was used by both North and South. Elmhurst (built in 1824) in Greenbrier County on the James River & Kanawha Turnpike was a rather grand establishment with twenty-four rooms. A Union officer ordered its evacuation and burning in 1864, but he rescinded that order when an army doctor confirmed that removing a seriously ill resident would cause her death. Traveller's Repose in Pocahontas County was the first stage stop west of the Allegheny Mountains on the Staunton–Parkersburg Turnpike, and it took twenty-four cannonball hits from the Union army during the Battle of Greenbrier River in October 1861. Traveller's Repose burned during the war but was rebuilt in 1866, continuing to serve as a stagecoach stop until the early 1900s.

A FAMILY BESIEGED

Both sides during the Civil War might use stagecoach taverns, warehouses, churches and fine homes for hospitals, barracks or headquarters, particularly those buildings that stood on strategic ground. When George Chancellor, an innkeeper in Spotsylvania County, advertised his tavern Chancellorsville in 1816, he made much of its location. It lay "directly in the forks of Eley's Road and the Turnpike"—a popular road to the mountains. He had acquired Chancellorsville as a gift from his brother-in-law. His wife, a widow named Ann (Lyon) Pound, had been keeping an ordinary nearby at Fairview, a squared log structure about half a mile away from where the new tavern would be built.

Chancellorsville was popular with all sorts of travelers, including the gentlefolk, politicians, students, backwoodsmen and wagoners. Travelers would make it their habitual stop on the way from Fredericksburg to the mountains in the west. It was found that the crushed stone over the sticky

Virginia clay was not enough to make the toll road an easy route, so in the 1850s, the Fredericksburg & Valley Plank Road, usually called Orange Plank Road, was finished to run from Fredericksburg to Orange Court House. Planking—eight feet long and three or four inches thick—was used over only half the roadbed, the side that carried heavily loaded wagons eastward from the Shenandoah Valley to market in Fredericksburg.

Plank roads became popular because their smooth wood surface was seemingly impervious to mud and coaches and their passengers. They also allowed traffic to move much more quickly. Road builders often manufactured the planks onsite, using steam-powered sawmills along the roadbed to build the plank road from wood sawn from nearby trees.

Chancellorsville's location had made its fortune in peaceful years, but the Civil War brought its doom. By this time, the tavern had passed into other family members' hands. At first, it continued to provide "well-bred entertainment," as Ralph Happel remarked in his article "The Chancellors of Chancellorsville," to the Confederate troops who were stationed nearby to guard the river.

That was a fairly peaceable time but truly the calm before the storm. The Battle of Chancellorsville (April 30–May 6, 1863) was a major battle in the Civil War. It would be a victory for the outnumbered Confederates due to the tactics of General Robert E. Lee, but Lee lost one of his best generals, Thomas "Stonewall" Jackson, who died of complications from his wounds.

The family who owned Chancellorsville was still in residence during the battle, and the structure was occupied by Union troops. The Chancellor women had hidden the silverware and a gold piece gifted to them by General J.E.B. (James Ewell Brown) Stuart in their hoop skirts. The hams were stashed under the front steps, and the corn crop was hidden under their beds. They stood the occupation fairly well, but Chancellorsville was turned into Union general Joseph Hooker's headquarters.

As the shelling increased, General Hooker ordered the civilians into the basement for their safety. Meanwhile, their sitting room was turned into an operating room, and the girls' piano became the amputating table. The Union surgeon let the Chancellor women tend two wounded Confederate soldiers who had ended up in their custody. To add to the misery, the basement started to flood. The Chancellors were given food—and whiskey, too, by doctor's orders. But worst was yet to come. Sue Chancellor, who was a young girl at the time, wrote her reminiscences later for the *Confederate Veteran* magazine in 1921:

Joseph Dickinson of Maine, brevetted for gallantry on staff duty at Gettysburg. *Courtesy of the Library of Congress.*

It was late that day when the awful time began. Cannonading on all sides and such shrieks and groans, such commotion of all kinds! We thought that we were frightened before, but this was beyond everything and kept up until after dark. Upstairs they were bringing in the wounded, and we could hear their screams of pain. This was Jackson's flank movement, but we did not know it then. Again we spent the night, sixteen of us, in that one room, the last night in the old house.

Early in the morning they came for us to go into the cellar, and in passing through the upper porch I saw how the chairs were riddled with bullets and the shattered columns which had fallen and injured General Hooker. O the horror of that day! The piles of legs and arms outside the sitting room window and rows and rows of dead bodies covered with canvas! The fighting was awful, and the frightened men crowded into the basement for protection from the deadly fire of the Confederates, but an officer came and ordered them out, commanding them not to intrude upon the terror-stricken women. Presently down the steps the san officer came precipitously and bade us get out at once, "for madam, the house is on fire, but I will see that you are protected and taken to a place of safety."

They escaped their burning home only to walk into a scene from a nightmare: "The woods around the house were a sheet of fire, the air was filled with shot and shell, horses were running, rearing, and screaming, the men a mass of confusion, moaning, cursing and praying. They were bringing the wounded out of the house, as it was on fire in several places."

Union general Joseph Dickinson, who had escorted them from the burning house, insisted on leading them to safety. He led them toward U.S. Ford and demanded a soldier on horseback give his mount to one of Sue's sisters, who had a hemorrhage in her lungs and could not walk. He escorted the family as far as the pontoon bridge, where he left them in the care of a chaplain but not before being stopped by a Union officer who demanded to know why he wasn't at his duty post. His reply: "If here is not the post of duty, looking after the safety of these helpless women and children, then I don't know what you call duty."

In the years after the war, General Dickinson and the Chancellor family remained close friends. He and Mrs. Chancellor wrote to one another often, and he would frequently stop to see her on his visits to the battlefields. He attended her funeral in 1892 out of "the affection he felt for her."

Chancellorsville was rebuilt about 1870, but it was destroyed by fire again in 1927. Today, those interested in the area's Civil War history can visit the National Park Service's Chancellorsville Visitor Center. But Chancellorsville itself is no more.

"The Army of the Potomac at Mine Run, Attacking Robertson's [Robinson's] Tavern, 1864." *Courtesy of the Library of Congress.*

TARDY AT ROBINSON'S TAVERN

At Locust Grove, not very far from Chancellorsville, there was another tavern that saw significant troop movement of both the Northern and Southern armies. Union general George Meade was trying to gather his army here for the Mine Run Campaign in November 1863, but one corps that arrived late changed his plans. The following May, Confederate general Richard Ewell camped his troops in the vicinity as he moved them east from Orange during the Wilderness Campaign.

As author Chris Mackowski related in his post "Robinson's Tavern Today," the building that housed the tavern still exists, although it has been moved about 250 yards north from its prime location next to the Orange Turnpike (Route 20) to make room for a small shopping area.

A CAVALRY CLASH AT THE BATTLE OF TODD'S TAVERN

Todd's Tavern lay on Brock Road in Spotsylvania County, a few miles from Chancellorsville. During the Battle of the Wilderness in May 1864, Major General Philip A. Sheridan, who would be responsible for burning much of the Shenandoah Valley later on in 1864, had held Todd's Tavern, but after he withdrew to Chancellorsville, Confederate major general Fitzhugh Lee reoccupied the area. Lieutenant General Ulysses Grant wanted it retaken for the Union, so Sheridan put two divisions on it, coming at the tavern from two different directions. This plan worked, but ultimately, after a fierce, long cavalry battle, the Confederates seized the tactical advantage and were able to reach the Spotsylvania battlefield first.

Todd's Tavern no longer stands. It was destroyed sometime before 1884.

GENERAL STUART KILLED AT YELLOW TAVERN

The Battle of Yellow Tavern (May 11, 1864) took place as part of the same Overland Campaign that included the Battle of the Wilderness. The name Yellow Tavern persists in Henrico County near Richmond, but the tavern itself is gone. In fact, it wasn't even an operating tavern when the war came to its door.

While Grant and Lee were otherwise occupied in Spotsylvania, General Philip Sheridan took twelve thousand cavalrymen to make a raid on Richmond, the capital of the Confederacy. Sheridan's troops encountered four thousand men led by Confederate general J.E.B. Stuart. Stuart fell mortally wounded in the attack, but Sheridan did not press on to Richmond, where local defense units lay in wait. Instead he rode around to join General Benjamin Butler's troops at Bermuda Hundred.

THE CROSSROADS AT COLD HARBOR TAVERN

Isaac Burnett was the proprietor at an inn that became better known as Old Cold Harbor Tavern. Writing for the *Richmond Times-Dispatch* at the sesquicentennial of the Battle of Cold Harbor in 2014, Isaac's great-great-grandson, Michael T. "Mickey" Reardon, relayed what happened when the Union came to the inn. Isaac Burnett's inn sat on his 182-acre farm. He was fifty-eight at the time and living with his wife, Sarah Hughes Burnett, who was fifty-one. They had thirteen children—nine daughters and four sons, one of whom, George, was serving in the Twenty-Fourth Virginia Cavalry. Isaac's daughter Martha, twenty-one

Cold Harbor Tavern, June 3, 1864. *By Edwin Forbes, courtesy of the Library of Congress.*

years old at the time of the battle, remembered: "In the month of June 1864, Gen. Grant's army came on the property and swept it clean in the way of supplies for man or beast."

Indeed, the Union soldiers made use of anything on the property, including dismantling (and hauling away) the stable, the corn house, the wagon house and the general-use house, as well as the property's fences—estimated at more than four thousand panels. They cut forty acres of timber and grazed their cattle and horses on the growing crops. As for the Burnett livestock, it was slaughtered onsite or taken for future use. In 1905, the family filed for damages from the U.S. government. Their claim was denied.

From May 31 to June 12, 1864, the crossroads at Cold Harbor Tavern was a key strategic position near the Confederate capital in Richmond, so naturally, both the North and South wanted it. One of its roads connected with the Pamunkey River and Grant's supply corridor. Cutting that connection would make it harder for the North to amass troops in the area. The Battle of Cold Harbor lasted nearly two weeks, costing thirteen thousand casualties—mostly on the Union side—and this after the bruising

Overland Campaign tallied an estimated fifty thousand Union casualties. Cold Harbor would ultimately be Lee's last large-scale field victory, followed by siege warfare at Richmond and Petersburg. After months of defense, the trench lines surrounding those cities would give way, and the end would be in sight.

LOMBARDY GROVE TAVERN

The Boydton–Petersburg Plank Road was the site of a battle on October 28–29, 1864, during the Siege of Petersburg. Lombardy Grove Tavern lay along it. The Confederate government had designated Lombardy Grove and Boyd's Tavern as recruiting stations. Lombardy Grove Tavern was also a salt disbursement site—salt, so crucial in the days before refrigeration, was rationed to twenty pounds per household so that the army could have enough for its needs. Initially, Lombardy Grove was owned during the war years by Joseph H. Jones. He sent a son to war who vanished into the North after having been taken prisoner on August 16, 1864, near Front Royal. Later, it was found that he had first been sent to Washington, D.C., and then to the prison in Elmira, New York, before being paroled.

Harwood A. Lockett was the tavern's second operator during the war years, and he eventually purchased it. His daughter, Myrta Lockett Avery, was the author of *A Virginia Girl in the Civil War* and *Dixie after the War*, among others. The books were reputed to have heavily influenced Margaret Mitchell in writing *Gone with the Wind*. The Lockett family owned Lombardy Grove until 1892. It is now a private residence.

AT APPOMATTOX

Due to their strategic locations at the intersections of major roads and convenient facilities, such as reliable wells, blacksmith shops and more, taverns were frequent backdrops for Civil War history right up to the very end. One old tavern, once also a home called Clover Hill, is now a prized part of the National Park Service's historic property at Appomattox Battlefield. It lies across the road from the McLean house, where General Lee signed the surrender, which was accepted by General Grant.

Clover Hill was only a shell of its former self when Ethel Marion Smith wrote it up for the *Virginia Magazine of History and Biography* in 1949, but the National Park Service had just acquired it then and restored it within the next decade.

Its history is quite interesting, and thanks to its restoration, it can be visited today. Clover Hill was both a private home and the center of a stagecoach depot whose route ran between Richmond, Lynchburg and Salem. The line was started by Alexander Patteson and his brother Lilbourn, with Alexander living at Clover Hill and conducting his business there until he died in 1836. Adjacent to Clover Hill was a guesthouse for stage passengers, and there were also slave quarters, an office and a blacksmith shop.

Ethel Smith, the great-granddaughter of Alexander Patteson, noted that he was both prosperous and pious (a Baptist) and provided money in his will for his slaves to be freed, which they were—in Ohio.

Initially, Clover Hill stood in Prince Edward County, but this section became part of Appomattox when that new county was formed in 1845. The stage property is listed as part of Alexander Patteson's estate, including "1 Troy coach, nearly new, with appurtenances complete, including 2 double and 4 single trees, $400." The inventory made at the time of his death also includes many particulars that would be necessary in a staging depot, including thousands of pounds of bacon, and Smith's article also mentions that the receipts to be made by the stage line from the mail contract brought about an eighth ($1,500) of what the passenger fares did ($12,773) in the year following Patteson's death.

Almost thirty years later, Clover Hill would be witness to the last moments of the Civil War as the South surrendered and the Confederates laid down their arms, and George Burnett, of Cold Harbor Tavern, would be of their number. On display in the old tavern in Appomattox are hundreds of facsimiles of paroles granted to the soldiers who began their journeys home.

XV

THE END OF THE LINE

TO MAKE CROQUETS

Take cold fowl or fresh meat of any kind, with slices of ham, fat and lean—chop them together very fine, add half as much stale bread grated, salt, pepper, grated nutmeg, a tea-spoonful of made mustard, a table-spoonful of catsup, and a lump of butter; knead all well together till it resembles sausage meat, make them in cakes, dip them in the yolk of an egg beaten, cover them thickly with grated bread, and fry them a light brown.

JUST THE TICKET

It was 1830, during the golden age for stagecoaches, when the small "Tom Thumb" locomotive chugged its way on the new Baltimore & Ohio (B&O) Railroad. It ran twelve miles in seventy-two minutes, and its passenger coaches looked very much like stagecoaches. It was trouble.

In March of the following year, the *Richmond Enquirer* detailed a debate in the Virginia legislature for its readers: what would it mean if the B&O Railroad extended all the way out to the Shenandoah Valley? The valuable trade would bypass Virginia markets and head to Baltimore instead. Clearly, Virginia needed to get in the railroad business, too. So the Winchester & Potomac Railroad was chartered in 1831. By 1837, it linked Winchester, Virginia, to Harpers Ferry, (West) Virginia, where there was a junction with

Virginia by Stagecoach

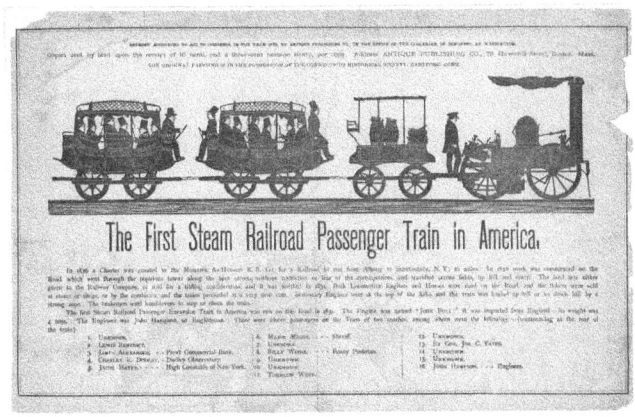

The first steam railroad passenger train in America, opened in 1831. *Courtesy of the Library of Congress.*

the B&O Railroad. There was worry on Virginia's part that most of the valley's produce might be shipped to sell in Baltimore or Philadelphia, so connections with the southern part of the Shenandoah Valley were not authorized. Those areas would have to be connected by other railroads, including the Manassas Gap Railroad, which connected at Manassas to the Orange & Alexandria Railroad, and the Virginia Central Railroad, which connected Staunton to Richmond.

Over the next 150 years, there would be dozens of railroads providing service throughout the Commonwealth. Compared to the stagecoaches, the railroads were relatively quick, certainly more comfortable and gave the impression of being much safer. The golden age for stagecoaches gave way to a golden age for locomotives, but stagecoaches were still necessary to make connections to areas that did not lie on rail lines.

STAGECOACHES GET SIDETRACKED

Then the railroads started to do business in "the turnpike counties." When the Manassas Gap Railroad crossed the Blue Ridge from Manassas to Mount Jackson, the nearby toll revenue dropped $14,000 in three years' time. The Valley Turnpike company directors tried to fight back and file an injunction to keep the railroad from being built too close to the turnpike, but they failed. By 1855, so many of the turnpike board members had invested in the railroad that they found they couldn't have a quorum for a turnpike board meeting if it conflicted with a railroad board meeting.

Adding salt to the wounds, the railroads were becoming not just popular freight movers but also people movers. And then the steam engines started getting the lucrative U.S. mail contracts instead of the stage lines.

To adjust to the new realities, stage lines had to cut back on their service areas, which meant business dried up for stagecoach inns, many of which closed—being converted to private residences or abandoned altogether. The development of the telegraph also cut into trade, as near-instant messaging did away with the necessity of carrying important business or personal communications by swift stagecoach. Still, up until the time of the Civil War, stagecoaches were really quite popular. Afterward, however, rail lines took over the business of transport from the main stage roads, leaving the stagecoaches as a secondary way to travel, at least in the eastern United States. The land west of the Mississippi, however, was opening up, and its wide-open spaces were an invitation for stagecoaches.

Railroads really took hold of the western part of Virginia and West Virginia in the 1870s, and that coincided with the coming of the coal industry. With railroads making shipping heavy loads long distances practical, the coal companies established themselves most naturally along rail lines. Company towns would concentrate near the mine and the railroad.

Interestingly, however, if you go to a major railroad museum today, such as the B&O Museum in Baltimore, you will probably find displayed among the mighty engines a stagecoach exhibit. Its presence is an acknowledgement

Old Tavern No. One, Winchester, 1933. *Courtesy of the Historic American Buildings Survey, Library of Congress.*

"Watching the Stage Go By at Snickers Gap, Virginia," 1900–1. *Photograph by Frances Benjamin Johnston, courtesy of the Library of Congress.*

of the link stagecoaches provided to the more rural areas that lay miles from a train depot, as well as giving visitors a close-up look at what came before—when horsepower was horse power.

The rise of the automobile in the early part of the twentieth century finished the job of putting stagecoaches out to pasture. Horses and horse-drawn vehicles were no longer welcome on the major roads, and automation of farm equipment got them out of the fields, too.

ALL ABOARD

Railroads brought the market closer to small communities. In 1884, the New York, Philadelphia & Norfolk Railroad came to the Birdsnest area on the Eastern Shore, and a community developed where there had not been one before. The railroad depot was convenient for shipping produce, and Birdsnest was one of the many Eastern Shore communities that set up a packing shed to take full advantage of the easy and direct line to the city markets.

"My Christmas Greeting." *Author's collection.*

People in towns eventually stopped anticipating the melodious sound of stage horns and listened for the screams of steam whistles instead. The train's faster, more mechanical rhythm became the daily underlying tempo of progress.

But memories of stagecoach days were kept alive in stories told and sometimes written down. The hardships were forgotten as the coach-and-four became the symbol of a simpler time. Each winter, cheerful images of stagecoaches could be found on Christmas and New Year's cards, conveying nostalgic greetings and wishes for fellowship with nary a trace of mud or broken wheels to be seen.

XVI
TRACES OF THE PAST YOU CAN VISIT TODAY

FRIED CHICKENS

Cut them up as for the fricassee, dredge them well with flour, sprinkle them with salt, put them into a good quantity of boiling lard, and fry them a light brown; fry small pieces of mush and a quantity of parsley nicely picked, to be served in the dish with the chickens; take half a pint of rich milk, add to it a small bit of butter, with pepper, salt, and chopped parsley; stew it a little, and pour it over the chickens, and then garnish with the fried parsley.

As the twentieth century clattered on, tangible reminders of the old stagecoach days met a variety of fates. A few coaches found their way to museums and private collections. Driving coach horses can still be enjoyed by those in a position to do so, and it's a wonderful spectator sport. As for the stagecoach stops and coaching inns, their futures would be determined by a number of factors. In the early 1900s, there was new interest in historic preservation of buildings as a way of keeping a connection with the past in a respectful way.

FINDING USES FOR OLD SPACES

If the building was handsome and could be converted to a private dwelling, it might be. If it was plain and a bit rough, it might not last another century, either through neglect or just wear and tear. If it was located on a still-

Top: Old stagecoach. *Courtesy of Momentmal/Pixabay.*

Bottom: "Travis House: Good Eating," Williamsburg, 1936. *By Elizabeth O'Neill Verner, Courtesy of the Library of Congress.*

busy intersection and it didn't catch someone's attention as being worthy of preservation, it would likely be pulled down to make room for something more practical. There are, however, a number of old stagecoach inns that have kept to their original hospitable purpose or found them again.

Travis House in Williamsburg, though never a stagecoach inn, found a new purpose several times over. It was originally a private dwelling—a "town house"—that was eventually used as a residence by the supervisor at Eastern State Hospital. Originally built and soon expanded as a home for Colonel Edward Champion Travis about 1765, Travis House was moved in 1929 to Duke of Gloucester Street in the Colonial Williamsburg area. There, it supplanted two other interesting but less attractive old buildings that were in rather sorry shape, a theater and the City Hotel, once very popular in their heyday. At its new location, Travis House hosted a colonial-style restaurant for tourists during the 1940s. A favorite recipe was Travis House cookies, a butterscotch meringue treat with pecans. Travis House was moved twice more, ending its wanderings back at its original site on France Street.

The following is a sample of places in Virginia that have a link to stagecoach days and can be visited today. Before setting off to see a property, it is wise to check its current hours.

AMERICA'S FIRST SPA, BERKELEY SPRINGS, WEST VIRGINIA

https://berkeleysprings.com/history-berkeley-springs/

Although filled with modern spa opportunities, by right of the 1776 law that established the town, you can still drink freely of the mineral waters and fill your jugs at the public fountain. You can also wade in ancient stone pools at its small state park. The town itself has numerous pleasant diversions in a beautiful mountain setting. Berkeley Springs was a favorite retreat for George Washington and his family in the 1760s.

B&O RAILROAD MUSEUM, BALTIMORE

http://www.borail.org/
http://www.borail.org//stagecoach.aspx

The train museum has made a place for a reproduction Concord stagecoach.

THE BOYD TAVERN, BOYDTON
http://boydtavern.net/history/

Dating to about 1790, Boyd Tavern, a national historic landmark, is open for tours several days a week, and you can also contact them to schedule a special tour.

CAR & CARRIAGE MUSEUM, LURAY CAVERNS
https://luraycaverns.com/attractions/the-car-carriage-caravan-museum/

If you are going to see the caverns, the admission for this museum is included in the price of the ticket. It is a trip back in time.

COLONIAL WILLIAMSBURG

"CW," as the students at William & Mary call it, is a must-see for many Virginia visitors. The foundation has recreated several taverns there both as historic sites and eateries, including Shield's Tavern, Chowning's Tavern, the King's Arms Tavern, the Raleigh Tavern and Christina Campbell's Tavern. The artisans in the historic area practice many colonial crafts, including ones that would pertain to the stagecoach lines. CW also offers carriage rides for an additional fee.
To make a reservation at a tavern: https://www.colonialwilliamsburghotels.com/dining/
To make a reservation for a carriage ride: https://www.colonialwilliamsburg.com/explore/carriage-rides

FRONTIER CULTURE MUSEUM, STAUNTON
http://www.frontiermuseum.org/

This sprawling museum area has recreated ca. 1700 rural buildings from England, Germany, Ireland, West Africa and America. Exhibits are located in two areas: the Old World and America. It includes the Ganatastwi Exhibit, representing how a small group of Native Americans might have been living west of the Blue Ridge around 1730.

GADSBY'S TAVERN, ALEXANDRIA
https://www.gadsbystavernrestaurant.com/
https://www.alexandriava.gov/GadsbysTavern

This very historic tavern operates both as a restaurant and a museum. The museum offers special tours and workshops.

THE GLEN FERRIS INN,
FAYETTE COUNTY, WEST VIRGINIA
http://glenferrisinn.com/

Although much remodeled for modern conveniences, what was once the Stockton Tavern still has its historic dining room, Stockton Hall, and an amazing view of the falls at the Kanawha River.

GLOUCESTER MUSEUM OF HISTORY, GLOUCESTER
https://www.gloucesterva.info/830/About-the-Museum

Built in the late eighteenth century, John New's Tavern, which was owned in 1802 by Phillip Tabb, eventually became a hotel and is now a museum showcasing Gloucester County's history. It is one of the few brick taverns to survive from that early period. It has won an historic preservation award.

THE GREENBRIER,
WHITE SULPHUR SPRINGS, WEST VIRGINIA
http://www.greenbrier.com/

This is the place where the Metternich held sway. Although thoroughly modern in many ways, including more recent buildings, it respects its long history, and guests may still "take the waters" as part of their spa treatments.

HANOVER TAVERN AT HANOVER COURTHOUSE
http://hanovertavern.org/

Patrick Henry's place of employment as a young man hosts dinners and theater events as well as offering a self-guided tour.

THE HOMESTEAD, HOT SPRINGS
https://www.omnihotels.com/hotels/homestead-virginia/property-details/history

The Homestead has been operating as a resort since 1764. European-style spa therapies began in the 1830s. Today, it is a modern, luxurious hotel that maintains many classic features.

HUNTER'S HEAD TAVERN, UPPERVILLE
http://www.huntersheadtavern.com/

Styled as an authentic British pub with an organic and local focus, the building itself dates to the 1700s.

THE INN AT MONTROSS, WESTMORELAND COUNTY
http://innatmontross.net/

This lovely old inn has had a many-storied life, having served as a tavern in stagecoach days. The current building dates to about 1800 and still serves and lodges travelers.

THE INN AT PROSPECT HILL, LOUISA COUNTY
http://www.prospecthill.com/

Located somewhat near the now privately owned Boswell's Tavern, Prospect Hill is part of the Green Springs National Historic District. Like many formerly prosperous families after the Civil War, the Overton family took in paying guests at Prospect Hill. The gracious house was built in 1732 and offers a variety of lodging as well as a restaurant. It is akin to what Noah Webster might have experienced when staying in private homes on his book tour.

KING AND QUEEN COUNTY TAVERN MUSEUM
http://www.kingandqueenmuseum.org/tavern-museum/

A relatively new museum in a rather old building, this is a labor of love from the community with limited hours.

LAFAYETTE INN & RESTAURANT, STANARDSVILLE
https://thelafayette.com

Built in 1840, the inn was a stopping place for travelers on their way to the mountains. Today's inn and restaurant preserve a historic atmosphere.

Above: The Lafayette Inn & Restaurant, Stanardsville, dating to 1840. *Photograph by Sabonarola, from Wikimedia.*

Left: The dining room of the Lafayette Inn & Restaurant in Stanardsville. *Author's photograph.*

LEMAIRE RESTAURANT (JEFFERSON HOTEL), RICHMOND
https://www.lemairerestaurant.com/

You will find lodging and food here somewhat in the style of the 1890s. The *Richmond Times-Dispatch* called it "a genteel trip back in time."

THE LOG HOUSE 1776, WYTHEVILLE
http://www.loghouse1776.com/

Fine dining in an eighteenth-century setting can be found off of what was once the Wilderness Road.

THE MARTHA WASHINGTON INN & SPA, ABINGDON
http://www.themartha.com/

A gracious family home, a girls' college, a wartime hospital and later housing for actors at the nearby Barter Theatre, including Patricia Neal, Ernest Borgnine and Ned Beatty, the "Martha" opened as a hotel in 1935 and has had many illustrious guests.

MICHIE TAVERN, CHARLOTTESVILLE VICINITY
http://www.michietavern.com/

In the early twentieth century, this commodious tavern was moved to a better location just a mile or two from Jefferson's Monticello. A favorite stop for tourists, it offers tours of the tavern as well as a lunch including fried chicken and other Southern specialties.

THE NORTH HOUSE MUSEUM (STAR TAVERN), LEWISBURG, WEST VIRGINIA
http://www.greenbrierhistorical.org/
https://www.theclio.com/web/tour/summary?id=278

Now owned by the Greenbrier Historical Society, the museum—which has also been a private residence and a girls' school—contains interesting eighteenth- and nineteenth-century artifacts, including a Conestoga wagon. It became the Star Tavern in 1830 and was popular with jurists and visitors to the springs.

OLD CHICKAHOMINY HOUSE, WILLIAMSBURG
https://www.oldchickahominy.com/

While not a historic structure, this restaurant with attached gift shop has the look and feel of a place that would have welcomed stagecoach travelers.

THE RED FOX INN & TAVERN, MIDDLEBURG
http://www.redfox.com/

Built in 1723 by Joseph Chinn, it was called Mr. Chinn's Ordinary. In 1887, Mr. Chinn's Ordinary became the Middleburg Inn, and, in 1937, it was renamed the Red Fox Tavern. The Stray Fox Inn, a historical building adjacent to the Red Fox, is a recent addition to the original inn. Each room is named for a famous person, place or event. George Washington was among its early visitors. It was also a favorite of Jacqueline Kennedy. It is still very much open for business.

RICE'S HOTEL/HUGHLETT'S TAVERN, HEATHSVILLE
http://www.rhhtfoundationinc.org/

Open to visitors, the historic tavern serves food and has historic crafts guilds, including a blacksmith and weaving/spinning, as well as carriages on display during special events.

THE RICHARD JOHNSTON INN, FREDERICKSBURG
https://www.therichardjohnstoninn.com/en-us

Dating to the beginning of the 1800s, this building survived the Civil War—with a few honorable scars—and was turned into an award-winning bed-and-breakfast in the 1980s. Set in the heart of the historic downtown area across from the visitors' center, its furnishings reflect its storied past.

THE RISING SUN TAVERN, FREDERICKSBURG
http://www.washingtonheritagemuseums.org/

Originally built as a residence by George Washington's brother Charles, this building served as a tavern prior to the Civil War and also as a stage stop and post office. The costumed guides give a very entertaining tour, and special events are offered throughout the year.

THE TAVERN RESTAURANT, ABINGDON
http://www.abingdontavern.com/history.htm

Built in 1779 to be used as a tavern and overnight inn for stagecoach travelers, it also served as a post office. In its time, it entertained many famous persons. It is now open as a fine dining restaurant with a European flair.

THE WAYSIDE INN, MIDDLETOWN
http://www.alongthewayside.com/

The Wayside Inn, once known as Wilkenson's Tavern, has been offering food and lodging since 1797 and lies along the Valley Pike. It was a stagecoach stop and relay station.

THE WINMILL CARRIAGE MUSEUM AT MORVEN PARK, LEESBURG
http://www.morvenpark.org/mansion
https://www.morvenpark.org/equestrian-center/driving.html

With over forty antique carriages, coaches, sleds and carts, Morven Park also hosts carriage driving competitions that are open to the public.

SOURCES

Anderson, Belinda. "North House Museum." e-WV: The West Virginia Encyclopedia. October 21, 2010. Accessed October 29, 2018. https://www.wvencyclopedia.org/articles/1694.

Bailey, Francis, et al. *Journal of a Tour in Unsettled Parts of North America, in 1796 & 1797*. London: Baily Bros., 1856. https://archive.org/details/journaloftourinu00bail/page/n6.

Ballard, Dr. Margaret B. "Early History of Monroe: James and John Crow." *Monroe Watchman*, November 27, 1969. http://web.hardynet.com/~bunnyhollow/graphics/Early%20History%20of%20Monroe%20County.PDF.

"The Battle of Todd's Tavern." National Park Service. March 31, 2012. https://www.nps.gov/frsp/planyourvisit/ttav.htm.

Chastellux, François Jean, Marquis de. *Travels in North-America, in the Years 1780–81–82*. New York: 1828. https://archive.org/details/marquistravels00chasrich/page/n5.

Combe, George. *Notes on the United States of North America during a Phrenological Visit in 1838-9-40, vol. 1*. Philadelphia: Carey and Hart, 1841. https://books.google.com/books?id=cr4TAAAAYAAJ&dq=george%20combe%20travel%20notes%20on%20the%20united%20states&pg=PP1#v=onepage&q&f=false.

Corker, Carol, and Leigh Lambert. "Lombardy Grove Tavern." *Southern Virginia Homefront*. 2014. http://sovahomefront.org/_site_lombardygrove.php.

Sources

Crookshanks, Barbara. "Downtown Hotels Abounded in the 19th Century" (blog). Central Rappahanock Regional Library. October 3, 2018. https://www.librarypoint.org/blogs/post/downtown-hotels/.

Dames & Moore. *Final Report: Historic Architectural Survey—Settlements, Villages and Towns of Northampton County, Virginia*. Richmond: Department of Historic Resources, 1996. https://www.dhr.virginia.gov/pdf_files/SpecialCollections/NH-021_AH_Survey_Northampton_County_1996_DM_report_Cost-Share.pdf.

Davis, William W.H. *History of Bucks County, Pennsylvania: From the Discovery of the Delaware to the Present Time, vol. 2*. New York: Lewis Publishing Company, 1905. https://books.google.com/books?id=7kgVAAAAYAAJ&source=gbs_navlinks_s.

Doody, David M., and Mary Miley Theobald. *Rivers and Roads: Transportation in Early America*. Williamsburg, VA.: Colonial Williamsburg Foundation, 2015.

Duncan, John M. *Duncan's Travels Through Part of the United States and Canada in 1818 and 1819*. New York: W.B. Gilley, 1823.

Farish, Hunter D. *Travis House Architectural Report, Block 13-2 Building 23-A Lot 159*. Williamsburg, VA: Colonial Williamsburg Foundation Library, 1990. http://research.history.org/DigitalLibrary/View/index.cfm?doc=ResearchReports%5CRR1290.xml.

Fisher, Terri, and Kirsten Sparenborg. *Lost Communities of Virginia*. Earlysville, VA: Albemarle Books, 2011.

Garcia, Angelica. "Newgate Tavern." *The Clio*. October 22, 2016. https://www.theclio.com/web/entry?id=27059.

Gordon, James W., Jr. "French Place Names in Virginia." *The Huguenot Society of the Founders of Manakin in the Colony of Virginia*. February 20, 2016. http://huguenot-manakin.org/manakin/VAplaces.php.

Guild, June. *The Black Laws of Virginia*. The Plains, VA: Afro-American Historical Association of Fauquier County, 1995. https://static1.squarespace.com/static/559ec31fe4b0550458945194/t/563d0b6fe4b00a793bb2c6d6/1446841199468/BLACK+LAWS+OF+VIRGINIA.pdf (excerpted).

Halfway House/Tyree Tavern. National Register of Historic Places Nomination Form. July 17, 1978. http://www.wvculture.org/shpo/nr/pdf/fayette/78002792.pdf.

Happel, Ralph. "The Chancellors of Chancellorsville." *Virginia Magazine of History and Biography* 71, no. 3 (July 1963): 259–77. http://www.jstor.org/stable/4246953.

Hennessy, John. "Charles Dickens in White Oak?" *Fredericksburg Remembered: Musings on History, Public History, and Historic Fredericksburg* (blog). August 6, 2010. https://fredericksburghistory.wordpress.com/2010/08/06/charles-dickens-in-white-oak/.

Hofstra, Warren R., and Karl Raitz, eds. *The Great Valley Road of Virginia: Shenandoah Landscapes from Prehistory to the Present.* Charlottesville: University of Virginia Press, 2010.

Holmes, Oliver W., and Peter T. Rohrbach. *Stagecoach East: Stagecoach Days in the East from the Colonial Period to the Civil War.* Washington, D.C.: Smithsonian Institution Press, 1983.

Howison, Robert Reid. "Duelling in Virginia." *William and Mary Quarterly* 4, no. 4 (1924): 218–44. doi:10.2307/1919281.

Johnson, Virginia C. "Kind Acts and Courage at Chancellorsville" (blog). Central Rappahannock Regional Library. November 18, 2018. https://www.librarypoint.org/blogs/post/kind-acts-and-courage-at-chancellorsville/.

Johnson, William Page, II. "The Race Field at Fairfax Court House." *Fare Facs Gazette: The Newsletter of Historic Fairfax City Inc.* 13, no. 2 (Spring 2016). http://www.historicfairfax.org/wp-content/uploads/2016/08/HFCI1302-2016.pdf.

Karnes, Debrarae. *The History of the Prince William County Waterfront.* Prince William, VA: Prince William County Planning Office, 1998. http://www.pwcgov.org/government/dept/planning/Documents/000586.pdf.

Kennedy, Joe. "Times Are Tough, But Tiny Crows Goes On." *Roanoke Times*, September 28, 1980. https://www.roanoke.com/times-are-tough-but-tiny-crows-goes-on/article_d1066730-1eda-5f87-bc95-8d0d10e61824.html.

Kimmons, Rebecca Halstead. "Glen Ferris Inn." e-WV: The West Virginia Encyclopedia. August 7, 2017. Accessed November 15, 2018. https://www.wvencyclopedia.org/articles/2120.

King, George H.S. "General George Weedon." *William and Mary Quarterly* 20, no. 2 (April 1940): 237–52.

Krick, Robert E.L. "Control of Cold Harbor Crossroads." American Battlefield Trust. https://www.battlefields.org/learn/articles/control-cold-harbor-crossroads.

Lathrop, Elise. *Early American Inns and Taverns.* New York: Tudor Publishing Company, 1946.

"Levi Pease: Stage Route and Transportation Innovator." July 23, 2013. https://connecticuthistory.org/levi-pease-stage-route-and-transportation-innovator/.

Sources

Mackowski, Chris. "Robinson's Tavern Today." *Emerging Civil War* (blog). November 30, 2018. https://emergingcivilwar.com/2018/11/30/robinsons-tavern-today/.

Madden, T.O., Jr. *We Were Always Free: The Maddens of Culpeper County, Virginia: A 200-Year History*. New York: Vintage Books, 1993.

"Marlin and Sewell." e-WV: The West Virginia Encyclopedia. December 7, 2015. https://www.wvencyclopedia.org/articles/1508.

Marryat, Frederick. *A Diary in America: With Remarks on Its Institutions*, vol. 2. Paris: A. and W. Galignani, 1839. https://books.google.com/books?id=Ozk9AAAAYAAJ&l.

Maurer, David. "An Era Ended as Stagecoach Driver Passed." *Daily Progress*, August 23, 2010. http://www.dailyprogress.com/lifestyles/an-era-ended-as-stagecoach-driver-passed/article_97b7c480-eba7-56cc-a139-cddc58af6b41.html.

Miller, Ann B. *"Backsights"—Essays in Virginia Transportation History*. Vol. 1: *Reprints of Series 1 (1972–1985)*. Richmond: Virginia Department of Transportation, 2001. http://www.virginiadot.org/vtrc/main/online_reports/pdf/11-r18.pdf.

Miller, Lewis. "The Party at Supper & Breakfast, Chapman Springs." *Sketchbook of Landscapes in the State of Virginia, 1853*. Encyclopedia Virginia. https://www.encyclopediavirginia.org/media_player?mets_filename=evr4113mets.xml.

Mingus, Scott L. *Confederate General William "Extra Billy" Smith, From Virginia's Statehouse to Gettysburg Scapegoat*. El Dorado Hills, CA: Savas Beatie, 2013.

Moffatt, L.G., and J.M. Carrière. "A Frenchman Visits Norfolk, Fredericksburg and Orange County, 1816." *Virginia Magazine of History and Biography* 53, no. 2 (April 1945): 101–23. http://www.jstor.org/stable/4245343.

Murphy, M'Layne. *Historic Virginia Inns: A Cook's Tour: A Collection of Treasured Recipes, Chef's Tips, and Inn Highlights*. Dallas: Cardinal Productions Inc., 1986.

Northampton Order Book No. 44, 1857–1865: 516–18. *Eastern Shore Stuff*. http://easternshorestuff.com/misc/david_nottingham_bull.htm.

Ostler, Rosemarie. "Trial by Stagecoach: Noah Webster's Prescient Book Tour Was an Exercise in Survival." *American History Magazine* (December 2017). http://www.historynet.com/noah-websters-trial-by-stagecoach.htm.

Pawlett, Nathaniel Mason. "A Brief History of the Roads of Virginia, 1607–1840." Charlottesville: Virginia Highway & Transportation Research Council, 1977 (revised November, 2003). http://www.virginiadot.org/vtrc/main/online_reports/pdf/78-r16.pdf.

Payne, Dale, and Bob Beckelheimer. *Tales and Trails from the Fayette Tribune.* Fayetteville, WV: 1991.

Pearson, Janet. *Taking the Waters: 19th Century Medicinal Springs of Virginia.* Online exhibit based on *The Mineral Springs of Western Virginia by William Burke.* Historical Collections at the Claude Moore Health Sciences Library. 2007. http://exhibits.hsl.virginia.edu/springs/.

Phillips, V.N. Bud. *Pioneers in Paradise: Legends and Stories from Bristol Tennessee/Virginia.* Johnson City, TN: Overmountain Press, 2002.

Randolph, Mary. *The Virginia Housewife or Methodical Cook.* Philadelphia: E.H. Butler, 1860. http://www.gutenberg.org/files/12519/12519-h/12519-h.htm.

Reardon, Michael T. "Cold Harbor: 'The Golgotha of American history.'" *Richmond Times-Dispatch,* March 5, 2014. https://www.richmond.com/news/local/hanover/mechanicsville-local/cold-harbor-the-golgotha-of-american-history/article_6daf54da-a3ad-11e3-a876-0017a43b2370.html.

Robinson, Ed. *Historic Inns of Southern West Virginia.* Mount Pleasant, SC: Arcadia Publishing, 2007.

"Route to D.C." An Article Courtesy of the Thomas Jefferson Encyclopedia. https://www.monticello.org/site/research-and-collections/route-washington-dc.

"Set the Way-Back Machine!" *Fit to Print: Dispatches from the Virginia Newspaper Project @ the Library of Virginia.* April 20, 2014. http://www.virginiamemory.com/blogs/fit-to-print/tag/swan-tavern/.

Sincock, J. Morgan. *America's Early Taverns: Food, Drink, Lodging and Hospitality along the Nation's Early Roadways.* Lebanon, PA: Applied Arts Publishers, 1992.

Smith, Marion Ethel. "Clover Hill. Early History of an Old Appomattox Landmark." *Virginia Magazine of History and Biography* 57, no. 3 (July 1949): 269–73. http://www.jstor.org/stable/4245634.

"Spirits, Stills, and Temperance: Tracing the History of Alcohol in Shenandoah County." Curated by Shenandoah County Library. http://archives.countylib.org/tour/tours/show/11.

"The Stone House, Manassas National Battlefield Park." April 9, 2019. https://en.wikipedia.org/wiki/The_Stone_House,_Manassas_National_Battlefield_Park.

"The Transportation Network of Alexandria." Virginia Places. http://www.virginiaplaces.org/transportation/alextrans.html.

"Urban Development: Lodging—Ordinaries and Taverns." Stafford County Museum. November 2013. http://staffordcountymuseum.com/

wp-content/uploads/2013/11/Urban-Development-Lodging-Taverns-and-Ordinaries.pdf.
Vineyard, Ron. "Stage Waggons and Coaches." Colonial Williamsburg Foundation Library Research Report Series RR0380. August 2000. http://research.history.org/DigitalLibrary/View/index.cfm?doc=ResearchReports%5CRR0380.xml.
Voight, Virginia. *Stagecoach Days and Stagecoach Kings*. Champaign, IL: Garrard Publishing Company, 1970.
Washington, George. *The Diaries of George Washington*. Edited by Donald Jackson and Dorothy Twohig. Charlottesville: University Press of Virginia, 1976–79. https://www.loc.gov/item/75041365/.
Wells, Mary Lou. *The Illustrated Guide to the Morab Horse*. Manning, SC: Holladay Publishing, 2009.
"Wetherburn's Tavern." Colonial Williamsburg Foundation. http://www.history.org/almanack/places/hb/hbweth.cfm.
Wise, George. *History of the Seventeenth Virginia Infantry, C.S.A*. Baltimore: Kelly, Piet & Company, 1870. https://books.google.com/books?id=AS77Cym7LL0C&dq.
Writers' Program of the Work Projects Administration in the State of Virginia. *Dinwiddie County: "The Countrey of the Apamatica."* Richmond: Whittet & Shepperson, printers, 1942. http://www.vagenweb.org/dinwiddie/apamatica/ch3.htm.
"Yates Tavern—Circa 1750." Pittsylvania Historical Society. https://www.pittsylvaniahistoricalsociety.org/yates-tavern.pdf.
"Yew Hill." Virginia Department of Historic Resources. April 4, 2018. https://www.dhr.virginia.gov/historic-registers/030-0060/.
Yorktown's Main Street: Historic Resource Study. Part 1, Yorktown's Main Street (From Secretary Nelson's to the Windmill). Chap. 4, "Development along Main Street (Lot by Lot)." National Park Service. January 22, 2010. https://www.nps.gov/parkhistory/online_books/colo/yorktowns_main_street/chap1-4.htm.

INDEX

A

Abingdon 137, 176, 178
African Americans
  Birdsnest Tavern 151
  Chapman Springs 113
  Freedman's Bureau 52
  Isaacs, James "Jinks" 136
  Madden family 115
  Mitchell, John, Jr. 141
  Ohio, emancipation 119, 163
  Richmond Planet 141
  slave auction block, Fredericksburg 119
  slavery 14, 26, 35, 113, 115, 118, 119, 151, 163
Alexandria 22, 23, 43, 67, 68, 69, 129, 173
Alleghany County 61, 109
Allegheny Mountains 49, 60, 134, 155
Appomattox 162
Avery, Myrta Lockett 162

B

Baltimore 16, 43, 44, 59, 92, 93, 129, 164, 165, 166

Blue Ridge Mountains 14, 49, 68, 72, 165
Boone, Daniel 83

C

Charleston, West Virginia 61, 72, 130, 131, 146
Charlottesville 37, 53, 136
Civil War
  Battle of Chancellorsville 156, 159
  Battle of Cold Harbor 160, 161, 162
  Battle of First Manassas 149, 150
  Battle of Yellow Tavern 160
  Clover Hill Tavern, Appomattox 162, 163
  Conway, Moncure Daniel 119
  Dickinson, General Joseph 158
  Elmhurst, Greenbrier County, West Virginia 155
  Exchange Hotel, Gordonsville 52, 153
  Lee, General Robert E. 156, 162
  Old Stone House, Manassas 150
  Sheridan, General Philip A. 159, 160
  Stuart, General J.E.B. 156, 160

INDEX

Todd's Tavern, Spotsylvania County 159
Tyree's Tavern/Halfway House 154
Tyree Stone Tavern, Fayette County, West Virginia 154
Clay, Henry 65, 66, 79, 81, 82, 106
coaches
   Concord 88, 89, 90, 91, 92, 93, 171
   Flying Machine 94
   safety coaches 92
   stage waggons 15, 16, 17, 22, 93, 95, 121, 128, 129, 134
   Troy 88, 92, 93, 163
Conway, Moncure Daniel 116, 118

D

Dickens, Charles 116, 118
drovers 61, 115
dueling 79, 81, 82

F

Fauquier County 49, 50, 69, 111
ferries 14, 15, 49, 73, 88, 94, 150
Fredericksburg 21, 22, 23, 28, 29, 30, 52, 53, 76, 78, 79, 83, 84, 116, 118, 119, 124, 138, 155, 156, 177, 178
French and Indian War 28, 29, 42, 48, 49

G

Gordonsville 35, 51, 52, 55, 72, 153
Great Valley 145
Great Valley Road 48, 145
Greenbrier County, West Virginia 61, 72, 105, 155

H

Hazard, Ebenezer 23, 43
Henry, Patrick 26, 28, 29, 33, 173
Holmes, Oliver Wendell, Sr. 15, 38, 44, 87, 101, 134

horses 10, 11, 13, 14, 17, 22, 29, 30, 46, 48, 56, 59, 93, 95, 96, 97, 98, 99, 100, 101, 124, 127, 129, 132, 133
Huguenots 140, 141

J

Jaw Bones Club 83
Jefferson, Thomas 26, 29, 32, 33, 35, 37, 39, 43, 52, 57, 69, 106, 109, 141
Jouett, Jack 37, 54

K

Kanawha River 61, 65, 66, 73
Kenton, Simon 82
King's Highway 22, 138

L

Latrobe, Benjamin Henry 43, 46

M

Madison, James 35, 43, 51, 106, 115
Marryat, Captain Frederick 122, 123
Maury, Matthew Fontaine 123
McCormick, Cyrus 147
Metternich, the 104, 105
Midland Trail 61, 65, 72, 130
Mitchell, John, Jr. 141
Mitchell, Margaret 162
Monticello 37, 53
museums
   B&O Railroad Museum, Baltimore 166, 171
   Boyd's Tavern, Boydton 172
   Car & Carriage Museum, Luray Caverns 172
   Colonial Williamsburg 172
   Frontier Culture Museum, Staunton 172
   Gadsby's Tavern, Alexandria 173
   Hanover Tavern 173

INDEX

King and Queen County Tavern Museum 174
Michie Tavern, Charlottesville vicinity 176
North House Museum, Lewisburg, West Virginia 64, 176
Rice's Hotel/Hughlett's Tavern, Heathsville 177
Rising Sun Tavern, Fredericksburg 178
Winmill Carriage Museum, Morven Park 178

N

National Park Service 142, 143, 158, 162, 163
National Road 38, 57, 127
Native Americans 48, 49
　Battle of a Thousand Slain 73
　Blue Jacket, chief of the Shawnee 73
　Buckongahelas, chief of the Lenape 73
　Cornstalk, chief of the Shawnee 61
　Little Turtle, chief of the Miami 72, 73
　Nemacolin, chief of the Delaware 59
　Northwest Indian War (1785–1795) 72, 83
　Shawnee tribe 73, 83

O

Old Northwest 72
Old Stone House 150

P

Petersburg 43, 46, 55, 133
Pittsylvania 55
plank roads 156
　Fredericksburg & Valley Plank Road/Orange Plank Road 156
Poore, Benjamin Perley 139
Portsmouth 43, 44, 45, 133

post office
　Fairfax City 67
　New Post (Fredericksburg) 21
　Old Taylor Hotel, Winchester 51
　Philadelphia 21
　Post Office Act of 1792 126
　Post Office Ordinance of 1782 45
　stagecoaches to carry mail 22
　Steele's Tavern, Augusta County 147
　Sublett's Tavern, Powhatan County 141
post riders 22, 23, 139

R

racetracks
　Bowling Green 43
　Boydton 56
　Centreville 60
　Fairfax Court-House 68
　Fredericksburg 29
　Petersburg 48
railroads 112, 165
　Baltimore & Ohio Railroad (B&O) 164, 165
　Manassas Gap Railroad 165
　Orange & Alexandria Railroad 165
　Winchester & Potomac Railroad 164
Randolph, John (of Roanoke) 46, 79, 81, 124, 128
Randolph-Macon College 128
Randolph, Mary 10
　apple fritters 87
　buckwheat cakes 144
　chicken pudding 132
　corn meal bread 120
　croquets, to make 164
　drop biscuit 140
　fayette pudding 42
　fried chickens 169
　ginger wine 25
　mint cordial 102
　peaches in brandy 19
　perch, to fry 113

INDEX

pound cake 11
sliced potatoes, to fry 149
sweet potato buns 94
tavern biscuit 75
Ratcliffe, Richard 67, 68
Richmond 14, 23, 24, 43, 44, 45, 49, 52, 72, 107, 111, 116, 128, 133, 136, 139, 141, 160, 161, 163, 165, 176
road building 13, 14, 115, 156
Rocky Mount, Virginia 151

S

Sewell Mountain, West Virginia 60, 61, 130
Shenandoah Valley 37, 48, 49, 50, 56, 102, 144, 145, 146, 156, 160, 164, 165
Sir Archy (racehorse) 46
Spotsylvania County 155, 159, 160
springs
  Berkeley Springs, West Virginia 109, 112, 171
  Blue Sulphur Springs 65, 105, 106
  Chapman Springs 111, 113
  Fauquier White Sulphur Springs 111
  Hot Springs, the Homestead 109, 112, 174
  Salt Sulphur Springs 110
  Sweet Sulphur Springs, "Old Sweet" 106, 107, 108
  Warm Springs 82, 103, 109, 112
  White Sulphur Springs, the Greenbrier 103, 105, 108, 112, 173
Stafford County 84, 100, 116, 119, 124
stagecoach drivers
  Isaacs, James "Jinks" 136
  Leonard, John 135
  Tate, Mary "Old Moll" 137, 138
  Wines, Jack 135
stagecoach proprietors
  Beltzhoover & Co. 92
  Butterfield, John 98
  Hoomes, John 43
  Patteson, Alexander and Lilbourn 163
  Pease, Levi 22, 23, 42, 66
  Smith, William "Extra Billy" 138
  Twiford, Robert 44
  Twining, Nathanel 42, 43
  Van Horn, Gabriel 43
stagecoach racing 125
stagecoach robberies 126, 137
Staunton 37, 49, 136, 145, 165
steamboats 116, 119, 125, 139, 146

T

tavern entertainments 18, 30, 32, 46, 48, 76, 78, 146
tavern keepers
  Armistead (woman) 46
  Berry, Joseph 49
  Boswell, John 35
  Burnett, Isaac 160
  Carter, Thomas O. 150
  Chancellor, George 155
  Crow, Colonel John 61, 62, 63, 64
  Earp, Caleb 68
  Gadsby, John 69
  Jones, Joseph H. 162
  Lane, William Carr 59
  Lauck, Peter 50
  Lockett, Harwood A. 162
  Madden family 115
  Marot, John 35
  Michie, William 54
  New, John 142
  Ratcliffe, Richard 67
  Shields, James 35
  Tabb, Phillip 173
  Taylor, Bushrod 51
  Tyree, William 154
  Tyree (woman) 154
  Wetherburn, Anne Marot Shields 35
  Wetherburn, Henry 35
  Wills, Lucy 143

Index

tavern licenses 15, 46, 66, 143
taverns, inns and ordinaries
   Arell's Tavern, Alexandria 71
   Beverage House, Middleburg. *See* Red Fox Inn, Middleburg
   Birdsnest Tavern, Northampton County 150, 151
   Boswell's Tavern, Louisa County 35
   Boyd's Tavern, Boydton 55
   Bromley's Tavern, Petersburg 48
   Chancellorsville, Spotsylvania County 155, 156, 159
   Chinn's Crossroads, Middleburg. *See* Red Fox Inn, Middleburg
   City Hotel, Williamsburg 171
   Clover Hill Tavern, Appomattox 163
   Cold Harbor Tavern 160, 161, 163
   Courthouse Tavern, King and Queen County 174
   Cuckoo Tavern, Charlottesville area 37
   D.S. Tavern, Charlottesville area 54
   Eagle Tavern, Charlottesville area 54
   Earp's Ordinary, Fairfax City 67
   Eastville Inn, Cape Charles 44
   Exchange Hotel, Gordonsville 52, 55
   Flounder Tavern, Alexandria 69, 71
   Gadsby's Tavern, Alexandria 69
   Glen Ferris Inn, Fayette County, West Virginia. *See* Stockton Tavern, Fayette County, West Virginia
   Gordon's Tavern, Gordonsville 51, 52
   Hanover Tavern 26, 28, 173
   Indian Queen Tavern, Fredericksburg 79
   Ivy Inn, Charlottesville area 54
   John New's Ordinary, Gloucester County 142
   Lafayette Inn, Stanardsville 175
   Lombardy Grove Tavern, Mecklenburg County 162
   Macon Tavern, Powhatan County 140
   Madden's Tavern, Culpeper County 115
   Martha Washington Inn & Spa, Abingdon 176
   Michie Tavern, Charlottesville area 53, 54, 176
   Miller Tavern, Fayette County, West Virginia 155
   Newgate Tavern, Centreville 59
   Old Crow Tavern, Alleghany County 61, 62, 63, 64
   Pinch-'em-Slyly Tavern, Charlottesville area 54
   Pride's Tavern, Petersburg 48
   Raleigh Tavern, Williamsburg 32, 33, 35, 78, 172
   Red Fox Inn, Middleburg 56, 177
   Red Lion Tavern, Winchester 50
   Rice's Hotel/Hughlett's Tavern, Heathsville 177
   Rising Sun Tavern, Fredericksburg 30, 53, 76, 178
   Robertson's Tavern, Mine Run. *See* Robinson's Tavern, Locust Grove
   Robinson's Tavern, Locust Grove 159
   Somerwell House, Yorktown 143
   Star Tavern, Lewisburg, West Virginia 64, 177
   Steele's Tavern, Augusta County 147
   Stockton Tavern, Fayette County, West Virginia 65, 173
   Sublett's Tavern, Powhatan County 141
   Swan Tavern, Charlottesville 37, 54
   Swan Tavern, Richmond 141
   Swan Tavern, Yorktown 142, 143
   Tavern Restaurant, Abingdon 178
   Taylor Hotel, Winchester 51
   Taylor House, Cape Charles. *See* Eastville Inn, Cape Charles
   Taylor's Tavern, Falls Church 149, 150
   temperance tavern, Stafford County 84
   Todd's Tavern, Spotsylvania 159, 160

INDEX

Traveler's Rest, Mineral County, West Virginia 59
Traveller's Repose, Pocahontas County, West Virginia 155
Traveller's Rest, Fredericksburg 78
Tyree Stone Tavern, Fayette County, West Virginia 154
Tyree Tavern/Halfway House, Ansted, West Virginia 65
Wayside Inn, Middletown 56, 178
Weedon's Tavern, Fredericksburg 28, 29, 30
Wetherburn's Tavern, Williamsburg 33, 35
Williams Ordinary, Dumfries 124
Yates Tavern, Pittsylvania County 55
Yellow Tavern, Henrico County 160
Yew Hill/Robert Ashby's Tavern/Shacklett's Tavern, Fauquier County 50
Temperance Movement 37, 83, 84
Three Chopped/Three Notch'd Road 14, 49, 54
Tidewater region 11, 22, 48, 50, 102, 141, 145
travelers' accounts
  Bailey, Francis (ca. 1796) 16
  Combe, George (1838) 134
  Dickens, Charles (1842) 116
  Duncan, John (1819) 121
  Fithian, Philip Vickers (1774) 17
  Hagner, Mary (ca. 1839) 63
  Janson, Charles W. (ca. 1800) 40
  Jeffries, Thomas E. (1870) 130
  Latrobe, Benjamin Henry (1796) 46
  Marryat, Captain Frederick (ca. 1837) 122, 123
  McCarty, Captain Page (ca. 1861) 63
  Melish, John (1812) 121
  Michel, Francis Louis (ca. 1701) 13
  Parkinson, Richard (ca. 1799) 134
  Power, Tyrone (1836) 122
  Twining, Thomas (1807) 95
  Wakefield (colonial) 18
Warville, Jacques Pierre Brissot de (1788) 38, 39, 93
Webster, Noah (1785) 128
Wise, John Sergeant (1862) 151, 153
turnpikes
  Barboursville (West Virginia) Tollhouse 73
  Fauquier & Alexandria Turnpike 69, 71
  Little River Turnpike 67, 68
  Old Northwest Turnpike 59
  Staunton–Parkersburg Turnpike 155
  Valley Turnpike 57, 145, 165, 178

W

Washington, George 23, 28, 29, 33, 49, 51, 57, 59, 60, 69, 71, 73, 106, 124, 129, 134, 171, 177, 178
Webster, Noah 128, 129
Weedon, George 28, 29, 30, 42
Williamsburg 21, 22, 26, 96, 97, 100, 171, 172
Winchester 50, 59, 145, 146, 164
women
  Armistead (tavern keeper) 46
  Avery, Myrta Lockett 162
  Boswell (John Boswell's widow) 35
  Burwell, Rebecca 32
  Chancellor, Sue 156
  Clark, Mary "Polly" 150
  Hagner, Mary 63
  Madden, Mary 115
  Madden, Sarah 115
  Randolph, Mary 10
  Smith, Ethel Marion 163
  Tate, Mary "Old Moll" 137, 138
  Tyree (innkeeper) 154, 155
  Wakefield (early English traveler) 18
  Wetherburn, Anne Marot Shields 35
  Wills, Lucy 143

Y

Yorktown 22, 30, 124, 142, 143

ABOUT THE AUTHOR

Virginia Johnson is the Digital Services Librarian at the Central Rappahannock Regional Library in Fredericksburg where she is the lead content writer for the regional history page of the library's website. She has a BA in anthropology from the College of William and Mary, a master's degree in library and information science from the University of Maryland at College Park, and is a member of Beta Phi Mu international honor society for library and information studies. She is the co-author of *Virginia Horse Racing: Triumphs of the Turf* from The History Press.

American stage coach. *From* The History of Our Country, *by Abby Sage Richardson, 1876, courtesy of the Library of Congress.*

Visit us at
www.historypress.com

www.ingramcontent.com/pod-product-compliance
Lightning Source LLC
Chambersburg PA
CBHW042139160426
43201CB00021B/2342